The Anticorruption Frontline
The Anticorruption Report
Volume 2

Alina Mungiu-Pippidi (editor)

The Anticorruption Frontline

The Anticorruption Report 2

written by
Alessandro Bozzini
Mihály Fazekas
Jana Gutierréz Chvalkovská
Lina Khatib
Lawrence Peter King
Alina Mungiu-Pippidi
Jiří Skuhrovec
Ruslan Stefanov
Alexander Stoyanov
István János Tóth
Boryana Velcheva
Andrew Wilson

Barbara Budrich Publishers
Opladen • Berlin • Toronto 2014

All rights reserved. No part of this publication may be reproduced, stored in or introduced into a retrieval system, or transmitted, in any form, or by any means (electronic, mechanical, photocopying, recording or otherwise) without the prior written permission of Barbara Budrich Publishers. Any person who does any unauthorized act in relation to this publication may be liable to criminal prosecution and civil claims for damages.

You must not circulate this book in any other binding or cover and you must impose this same condition on any acquirer.

A CIP catalogue record for this book is available from
Die Deutsche Bibliothek (The German Library)

The information and views set out in this publication are those of the author(s) only and do not reflect any collective opinion of the ANTICORRP consortium, nor do they reflect the official opinion of the European Commission. Neither the European Commission nor any person acting on behalf of the European Commission is responsible for the use which might be made of the following information.

© 2014 by Barbara Budrich Publishers, Opladen, Berlin & Toronto
www.barbara-budrich.net

ISBN 978-3-8474-0144-5 (Paperback)
eISBN 978-3-8474-0276-3 (e-book)

Das Werk einschließlich aller seiner Teile ist urheberrechtlich geschützt. Jede Verwertung außerhalb der engen Grenzen des Urheberrechtsgesetzes ist ohne Zustimmung des Verlages unzulässig und strafbar. Das gilt insbesondere für Vervielfältigungen, Übersetzungen, Mikroverfilmungen und die Einspeicherung und Verarbeitung in elektronischen Systemen.

Die Deutsche Bibliothek – CIP-Einheitsaufnahme
Ein Titeldatensatz für die Publikation ist bei Der Deutschen Bibliothek erhältlich.

Verlag Barbara Budrich Barbara Budrich Publishers
Stauffenbergstr. 7. D-51379 Leverkusen Opladen, Germany

86 Delma Drive. Toronto, ON M8W 4P6 Canada
www.barbara-budrich.net

Jacket illustration by Bettina Lehfeldt, Kleinmachnow, Germany –
www.lehfeldtgraphic.de
Printed in Germany on acid-free paper by
Strauss GmbH, Mörlenbach, Germany

Contents

Executive summary 7

1. Ukraine: the New Sick Country of Europe 16
2. Bulgarian Anti-Corruption Reforms: a Lost Decade? 25
3. The Unlikely Achiever: Rwanda 40
4. Doubts and Lessons Learned from Qatar's Progress
   Towards Good Governance 51
5. Are EU Funds a Corruption Risk? The Impact of EU Funds
   on Grand Corruption in Central and Eastern Europe 68
6. Why Control of Corruption Works - When it Does 90

Appendix 124

Acknowledgements 128

Authors

Alessandro Bozzini is a researcher who was commissioned by with GIGA German Institute of Global and Area Studies for this study. He previously worked as a technical advisor to both Transparency International and the Deutsche Gesellschaft für Internationale Zusammenarbeit (GIZ) in Rwanda, (alessandrobozzini@gmail.com).

Mihály Fazekas, PhD, is a Post-Doctoral Researcher at the University of Cambridge, UK, (mf436@cam.ac.uk).

Jana Gutierréz Chvalkovská is a PhD student at the Institute of Economic Studies, Faculty of Social Sciences, Charles University, Prague, Czech Republic, (jana.chvalkovska@gmail.com).

Lina Khatib, PhD, is Director of the Carnegie Middle East Center in Beirut, Lebanon, (lkhatib@carnegie-mec.org).

Lawrence Peter King, PhD, is Professor of Sociology and Political Economy at the University of Cambridge, UK, (lk285@cam.ac.uk).

Alina Mungiu-Pippidi, PhD, is Professor of Democracy Studies at the Hertie School of Governance and Director of the European Research Centre for Anti-Corruption and State-Building, Berlin, Germany, (pippidi@hertie-school.org).

Jiří Skuhrovec is a PhD student at the Institute of Economic Studies, Faculty of Social Sciences, Charles University, Prague, Czech Republic, (jskuhrovec@gmail.com).

Ruslan Stefanov is Director of the Economic Program at the Center for the Study of Democracy, Sofia, Bulgaria, (ruslan.stefanov@online.bg).

Alexander Stoyanov is Director of Research at the Center for the Study of Democracy, Sofia, Bulgaria, (alexander.stoyanov@vitosha-research.com).

István János Tóth, PhD, is Co-director at the Corruption Research Center, Budapest, Hungary, (tothij@econ.core.hu).

Boryana Velcheva is an Analyst in the Economic Program at the Center for the Study of Democracy, Sofia, Bulgaria, (boryana.velcheva@onlin.bg).

Andrew Wilson, PhD, is Reader in Ukrainian Studies at University College, London, UK, (tjmsalw@ucl.ac.uk).

All these contributions were given as part of the European Union Seventh Framework Research Project ANTICORRP (Anti-corruption Policies Revisited: Global Trends and European Responses to the Challenge of Corruption). The views expressed in this report are solely those of the authors and the European Union is not liable for any use that may be made of the information contained therein.

Executive Summary

From Turkey to Egypt, Bulgaria to Ukraine, and Brazil to India, we witness the rise of an angry urban middle class protesting against what they see as fundamental corruption of their political regimes, perceived as predatory and inefficient. Corruption is near the top of all global protesters' list of grievances – from the Occupy movement to the Arab Spring. Their countries have benefited to varying degrees from globalization, but their regimes have all failed to evolve politically to meet their expectations. Corruption has become the main explanation for failures in government performance, for networks of patrons and clients subverting fair competition, and for billions of Euro in disappearing public funds, national or foreign assistance income. The economic crisis exposed the hypocrisy of rich countries which control corruption at home but use it to advance their economic interests abroad. The rise in the last two decades of an international anti-corruption regime only raised awareness but failed so far to diminish corruption. There is increasing demand for good governance resulting in quality education and health systems, and denunciation of sheer bread and circus populism. Briefly put, governments unable to control corruption cannot get away with organizing football World Cups anymore.

Volume 2 of the ANTICORRP Anticorruption Report tackles these issues across key cases and developments. The report is grouped into three parts:

1. The frontline reports, tracing developments in Ukraine and Bulgaria, where people rebelled against corrupt leaders, plus Rwanda and Qatar, who advanced in good governance charts, but find themselves accused of sponsoring wars across borders or bribing FIFA officials;
2. The methodology to move beyond perception-based corruption indicators, in the form of a three-country study on procurement data which reveals how EU funds increase the risk of corruption in Central Europe;
3. The empirical evidence on why control of corruption works when it does, and does not work for the most part, in the shortened version of ANTICORRP's first milestone report.

Chapter 1 In Chapter 1, **Andrew Wilson** discusses Ukraine whose February 2014 uprising was both caused by, and helped reveal, the extent of corruption in the country. Estimates are now that President Yanukovych and his circle stole $100 billion in just under four years. Ukraine has always been a badly-governed neo-patrimonial state; corruption has been endemic since independence in 1991. Ukraine's corruption is a post-Soviet legacy and has its roots in a failed transition, which multiplied resources for corruption instead of reducing them. Gas is at the heart of the problem, as most rich people in Ukraine made their money on subsidised Russian gas. Gas is to Ukraine like cocaine was to Colombia. Until the Orange Revolution in 2004, Ukraine received massively subsidised Russian and Central Asian gas at $50 per 1,000 m^3, when its average level of imports was 60 billion m^3 per annum (Ukrainian heavy industry is hugely energy-inefficient). In January 2006 Russia engineered a gas cut-off to punish the leaders of the Orange Revolution, and the price was controversially forced up to $230, though mixed with Central Asian gas it was discounted to $95 in a corrupt scheme. Only in 2009 did Ukraine agree to market prices, after another cut-off in the depth of winter, with the price rapidly topping $400. From 1991 to 2009, therefore, a massive gas subsidy was corruptly divided between Ukrainian and Russian politicians, at the expense of taxpayers in both states. Businesses still divert huge amounts of gas that is nominally supplied to households at a quarter of the import price (Ukrainian households supposedly consume two and a half times more gas than their richer Polish equivalents). Ukrainian companies like Oil and Gas of Ukraine have therefore built up huge debts, also because oligarchs used them for slush funds and covert funding of political projects.

The challenge for Ukraine now is how to put its house in order, as Russia claims it is basically a 'failed state'. How can the country at last enter a virtuous circle to avoid that after pushing down a neo-patrimonial regime a regime of competitive clientelism follows? Ukraine is presently the most problematic case of a corrupt order in Europe, and the EU does not have much experience in changing such regimes. Italy and Greece are living proof of how difficult governance is to change even under beneficial external influence - and Ukraine is subject to conflicting influences and major existential threats.

Chapter 2, on Bulgaria, argues that corruption is a key element to understand the Bulgarian governance regime, i.e. the way political and administrative power are acquired, used, structured, delegated and reproduced. The Worldwide Governance Indicators show that Bulgaria has made significant progress in the area of 'control of corruption' since 1996. This finding contrasts with the general opinion of the Bulgarian population who perceive Bulgarian institutions as corrupt, and contradicts the decision of the European Commission to continue monitoring Bulgaria's progress in fighting corruption and organized crime. Currently the governance regime of Bulgaria can best be described as having moved gradually from patrimonialism towards open access order, but most of its features are still in the competitive particularism stage when various power factions compete for spoils. Bulgarian governance has progressed since 1998 in particular as relates to administrative (petty) corruption, but it is has not yet evolved into an open access order. The indicators in the report are mostly from the area of public procurement. Despite the volume of the available government public procurement budget having declined since the crisis began, thus limiting the opportunities for corruption somewhat (European funds grew in volume as compensation), the two biggest public procurers, the energy and healthcare sectors, have opaque practices and remain vulnerable. Approximately 40% of all procedures for the awarding of public procurement contracts in the energy sector for 2012 were non-competitive, encompassing the various negotiated procedures with or without the publication of a contract notice under the 2004 Act on Public Procurement (APP). If the contracts awarded without any public procurement procedure are added to this number, it becomes apparent that avoiding market competition is the rule rather than the exception in the Bulgarian energy sector.

Chapter 3 analyses Rwanda, a country which has been praised by a large number of donors and development experts for its recovery from the 1994 genocide, sustained economic growth and improvement of many socioeconomic indicators, partly achieved thanks to massive aid flows. A key feature of Rwanda's progress is often considered to be governance and particularly anti-corruption: the country is generally regarded as one of the least corrupt in Africa and a success story in reducing corruption. This chapter analyses the state of corruption and the wider governance context in Rwanda, attempting to evaluate whether the country's governance regime is an open access order characterized by ethical universalism, a limited access order dominated by particularism, or a hybrid.

The author uncovers an important indicator, namely the presence of private companies who are dominant in the public contracts market and have close ties to rulers. Three holdings, or conglomerates, of 'party-statals', exist in Rwanda, although their connections with their stakeholders are not transparently stated on their websites. The largest one belongs to the government party (Crystal Ventures Limited (CVL), formerly known as Tri-Star Investments), which grew out of the production unit of the then-rebel army RPA during the 1990-94 war, which eventually put an end to the Genocide. Tri-Star got the bulk of its initial funding from wealthy supporters from the Rwandan diaspora. Today, CVL holds a majority stake in 11 companies and a minority stake in several joint ventures, ranging from civil works to real estate, telecommunications and security services, most of which are the leading national company in their sectors. The group's 2009 turnover represented over 3% of Rwanda's GDP. The second conglomerate, Horizon Group Limited, is often referred to in Kigali as 'the army's company.' The third consortium is Rwanda Investment Group (RIG), a holding company created in 2006 at the instigation of the Government, which is now a holding with both public and private shareholders whose purpose is to raise funds to invest primarily in the construction and energy sectors. There is a general perception among many local and foreign entrepreneurs that CVL and Horizon companies enjoy preferential treatment when they compete for public contracts. Given that Rwanda is practically a one-party state, the electoral as well as market domination raises serious doubts about the capacity of impartial distribution of public goods. Rwanda's top achievement remains control of petty bribery, an accomplishment which distinguishes the country in its geographic region.

Chapter 4

Chapter 4 explores the case of Qatar, a country recently showcased by international anti-corruption indices to be among the highest performing countries in the Middle East and North Africa. How can this be when Qatar is a neo-patrimonial absolute monarchy in which the state is not immune from private interests, and where the ruling family can bypass the rule of law? ANTICORRP author **Lina Khatib** looks for indicators to understand Qatar in the areas of public-private separation and allocation of public resources. Here Qatar emerges as a very special case since there is no real separation between the state and the private interests of the ruling family. There are no lobbies, no government watchdogs, no independent civil society, and freedom of the press is restricted when it comes to addressing internal affairs. Instead, citizens air their grievances through a traditional 'majlis' with tribal leaders, where people can submit petitions. However, conflicts of interest and the wealth of individuals are not scrutinised. There is also no transparency in public procurement. There is an official procurement process in place as well as regulations regarding conflicts of interest; but direct contracting is allowed in case of 'urgency' and seems frequent. However, several top down reforms have cut red tape and increased predictability.

Public allocation in Qatar follows a rentier system. State wealth is subject to distribution, with the existence of a welfare state that increases dependence on foreign expatriates to be the real work force, while Qatari nationals take state distributions for granted. While non-citizens pay for health care, electricity, water, and education, those services, in addition to housing, are provided to citizens for free. Fuel is subsidized for businesses as well as citizens, and Qatari businesses and agriculture also receive capital, electricity, and water subsidies. This makes Qatar a very special case.

The complete control by the monarch of state institutions and policies leaves no space for bottom-up calls for reform, or for independent assessment of the performance of the state and the actions of the ruling family by civil society and the media. The permeation of informal networks within state institutions and civil society, the lack of interest in and avenues for political participation among Qatari citizens, and the clientelistic relationship between citizens and the state support the continuation of this status quo. The chapter concludes that the absence of certain types of information on Qatar in the first place casts a shadow of doubt over the performance of the country in anti-corruption indices.

Chapter 5 explores the impact of EU structural funds on institutionalised grand corruption in three countries where corruption is systemic – Czech Republic, Hungary, and Slovakia – between 2009-12. By exploiting a unique pooled database containing contract-level public procurement information for all three countries, ANTICORRP researchers were able to systematically examine corruption risks associated with EU funding at the micro-level.

Developing comparative indicators of institutionalised grand corruption in public procurement for all three countries represents the primary methodological innovation of this article. The approach closely follows the composite indicator building methodology developed by the authors and introduced previously in ANTICORRP reports through the **work of author Mihály Fazekas.** It is based on a **data mining technique** making use of a wide range of public procurement 'red flags'.

The measurement approach exploits the fact that **for institutionalised grand corruption to work, procurement contracts have to be awarded recurrently to companies belonging to the corrupt network**. This can only be achieved if legally prescribed rules of competition and openness are circumvented. By implication, it is possible to identify the input side of the corruption process, that is techniques used for limiting competition (e.g. leaving too little time for bidders to submit their bids), and also the output side of corruption, that is signs of limited competition (e.g. single bid received and recurrent contract award to the same company). By measuring the degree of unfair restriction of competition in public procurement, a proxy indicator of corruption can be obtained. This indicator, called **corruption risk index (CRI) represents the probability of particularistic contract award and delivery in public procurement** falling between 0 and 1.

Regression results indicate that there is considerable market access restriction, hence likely institutionalised grand corruption, going on in all three countries during the 2009-12 period, by and large following the same techniques and 'tricks'. These results on their own demonstrate that corruption is systemic in public procurement in these countries. The reaching of robust regression models with considerable explanatory power by using the same regression set-up and variables point at the feasibility of cross-country measurement.

For instance, in the **Czech Republic**, the modification of the call for tenders is associated with a 0.6% higher probability of receiving a single bid and with a 1.5% higher winner's contract share. Both results point at a likely interpretation that modifying the call for tenders during the bidding phase is systematically used for restricting access and recurrently benefiting the same company. This result warrants making the modification of call for tenders part of the Czech CRI. In **Slovakia**, not publishing the call for tenders in the official journal is associated with 9.0% higher probability of a single bidder contract award and a 1.3% higher winner's contract share. Both results suggest that avoiding the transparent and easily accessible publication of a new tender can typically be used for limiting competition to recurrently benefit a particular company. This means that calls for tenders not published in the official journal becomes part of the Slovak CRI. In **Hungary**, leaving only 5 or fewer days, inclusive the weekend, for bidders to submit their bids is associated with 20% higher probability of a single bidder contract and with a 7.9%

higher winner's contract share compared to periods longer than 20 calendar days. These indicate that extremely short submission periods are often used for limiting competition and awarding contracts recurrently to the same company.

The chapter ultimately concludes that EU funding impacts institutionalised grand corruption in the three countries in two ways: first, by providing additional public resources available for corrupt rent extraction; second, by increasing the controls of corruption for the additionally allocated funding. Their preliminary calculations indicate that the first effect increases the value of particularistic resource allocation in the three countries up to 1.21% of their GDPs, while the second effect decreases the value of particularistic resource allocation by up to 0.03% of GDP.

Chapter 6

Chapter 6 is based on the largest and most substantial report of ANTICORRP so far. It explores why some societies manage to establish control of corruption and others not. Control of corruption is defined by **author Alina Mungiu-Pippidi** as the **capacity of a society to constrain individual corrupt behaviour (defined as particular distribution of public goods leading to undue private profit) in order to enforce the norm of individual integrity in public service and politics as well as to uphold a state that is free from capture by particular interests and able to promote social welfare**. This shortened version of the ANTICORRP milestone report explains the causes of the global fight and stagnation against corruption. It uses 2013 data to explain why societies around the world that feel their governments act for their self-interest alone call this corruption.

The main research question is addressed from an interdisciplinary perspective and by a large-N comparison method. For the dependent variables, the report uses: the aggregated Control of Corruption Index (CoC) from the World Bank, the Corruption Risk Index from the International Country Risk Guide (ICRG), the experience with bribe and perception of official's corruption from the Global Corruption Barometer 2013, the experience with bribe and perception of favouritism from ANTICORRP's own QOG 2013 European survey, the expert perception of diversion of public funds from the World Economic Forum Global Competitiveness Survey and the tolerance towards corrupt practices from the World Values Survey 2008. The full version can be read at http://anticorrp.eu/publications/quantitative-report-on-causes/. The report finds that individual behaviour is predicted by context (most people simply follow the 'rules of the game' in their own societies) and individual status (individuals who believe in competition more due to their individual skills tend to be less tolerant towards corruption). Societal control of corruption is reached as a state of equilibrium between opportunities or resources (power discretion and potential spoils such as natural resources) and legal and normative constraints (checks and balances, collective action capacity of enlightened citizens). A parsimonious model based on this concept proves robust to testing and opens the possibility to calculate country risk and areas of vulnerability on more objective grounds than was possible until now. Institutional 'silver bullets' prove, on the contrary, disappointing and only the interaction between civil society and various tools of transparency seems to work. By and large the report fulfilled these objectives:

First To propose and bring solid evidence in favour of a holistic approach to control of corruption as a governance order. The report brings evidence that control of corruption is an equilibrium involving both state and society, widely perceived by respondents in highly salient opinions and attitudes which inform their behaviour. The various forms and types of corruption should be seen only as symptoms of a systemic vicious equilibrium, which can vary from one context to another according to individual resistance but which do not change the definition and mechanism of the equilibrium as a whole. It is highly unlikely that a radical change can work other than by a systemic approach.

> **Second**

To show that determinants of control of corruption are similar across measurements from very different sources, businesspeople, ordinary citizens and experts therefore validating the measurements of corruption. For the first time in anti-corruption research a similar model explaining control of corruption is tested across three different sources of data and proves similar and robust.

> **Third**

To propose a policy-relevant model able to explain most variance without resorting, like many models of 'institutional quality', to legacies such as age of democracy, colonial past, legal tradition and religion. All elements of the model can be influenced by human agency – if not by the agency of governments uninterested in changing the status quo then by the agency of civil society and international donors.

> **Fourth**

To test anti-corruption devices and prove which ones seem to work, and in what circumstances. Institutional weapons such as freedom of information acts work if institutional warriors exist and pick them up. Many interventions would gain in effectiveness if the stakeholders (taxpayers, consumers, businesses, NGOs) were to be involved, because **what works to deliver change is the interaction between civil society and the tool itself (for instance, fiscal transparency).** Anti-corruption policies should by default involve stakeholders and be reviewed by them, not formally and marginally, as in many pseudo social accountability designs, but substantively, in the whole policy cycle - the planning, implementation and evaluation of policies. None of the anti-corruption tools - existence of an anti-corruption agency or of an ombudsman, for instance - predict if a country has superior control of corruption or has progressed since its adoption compared with other countries which do not enjoy such tools.

A forecast based on this statistical model would imply that change in governance order can occur only gradually and by a succession of radical actions and disequilibria until a new equilibrium is achieved with better control of corruption. That explains why so few success stories have existed over the past twenty years and why they seem to result more from domestic agency and broad reforms (Estonia, Georgia, Uruguay) than from typical anti-corruption strategies focused on repressive agencies promoted by external donors.

> **Methodological recommendations**

Second generation indicators, unrelated to perception indicators and sensitive to change and policy intervention are a main objective of ANTICORRP so most reports on the first two years of the project design and test some indicator or another (full reports for many countries more can be read at http://anticorrp.eu/anticorrp-publications/). This selection offers a wide variety, such as indicators based on data collection (e.g. the Bulgarian report has an excellent example in the ratio of the total volume of the concluded public procurement contracts/ volume of the nationally audited public procurement contracts/ volume of the public procurement contracts with discovered violations, which shows beyond doubt that irregularities are the norm and not the exception in Bulgarian procurement). Reports on Rwanda, Botswana and Qatar draw on more qualitative indicators, while the report on Central European procurement is based on big data and advanced inferential statistics. By and large, indicators advanced by ANTICORRP manage to answer the main diagnosis questions, if corrupt transactions are occasional or rather the rule of the game - also the essential question in choosing an appropriate policy response.

On the basis of our work on indicators we have developed the following recommendations:

On corruption indicators' reliability and validity

The 'success stories' according to governance charts (World Bank and Corruption Perception Index) are largely not confirmed by the ANTICORRP reports on Rwanda and Qatar. These case studies suggest that the methodology used in the corruption indices is likely to have a biased impact on scores. Transparency International's Corruption Perception Index (CPI), World Governance Indicators (WGI), and the Global Competitiveness Index (GCI-which have rated Qatar highly in terms of anti-corruption measures-all partially rely on surveys or interviews with respondents from the resident business community who are asked about their perceptions rather than about in-country practices. The WGI also includes subjective assessments from non-governmental organizations and public sector bodies. However, in the case of Qatar, the former are not independent from government influence and the latter are controlled by the ruling family. The case in point is revealed by looking at measures of independence of the judiciary as revealed by those indicators, compared with results from the Human Rights Dataset, which relies on Amnesty International reports and the State Department's Country Reports on Human Practices - i.e., indicators of practice rather than perception as sources.

The ANTICORRP analysis reveals that the specific indicators conventionally used to measure anti-corruption are incomplete, due to nuances not covered by those indicators. In their approach to what constitutes corruption, anti-corruption indices focus on bribery but miss measuring if social allocation is based on ethical universalism (people treated similarly) or not. Therefore, particular questions need to be asked to get a fuller picture of corruption and anti-corruption in a given country. Those questions would try to establish:

- Is there public information about public expenditure? How transparent is public procurement?
- Where do sources of information on corruption come from? Is there a freedom of information act? If information mostly comes from the government and the media are not free to report on corruption, a positive governance ranking should be questioned.
- Where do anti-corruption initiatives come from? Are there any non-governmental anti-corruption initiatives?
- Is there a monitoring and accountability framework so that people know what is going on in their government? If there is no watchdog to measure government performance and hold it accountable it is very unlikely governance can be so good.
- How is corruption defined? In Qatar and Rwanda, corruption seems to be narrowly defined as being solely about bribes, while social connections linked with privileged allocation are widely accepted. The paradox then emerges of patrimonial states being rated 'clean' by corruption ratings.

Corruption should always be defined in broad terms as encompassing all its forms, including non-monetary ones, as a country might have low incidence of some forms and high incidence of others. Moreover, the case of Rwanda suggests that petty or administrative corruption can in some cases be a very different issue from grand or political corruption, as curbing the former does not necessarily mean reducing the latter.

In addition, and perhaps most importantly, Qatar and Rwanda shows that relative success in fighting bribery is not necessarily associated, as many would assume, with high levels of accountability, transparency and citizen participation. This confirms the need, when investigating corruption, to analyse the broader governance context of a country.

On alternatives to corruption indicators

The ANTICORRP work on social allocation indicators provides a country specific, non-perception based data collection method which can add to or replace perception based governance indicators. In the particular case of EU funds this can be achieved by the introduction of an EU-wide, real-time monitoring mechanism of EU funds spending designed to detect systematic fraud and corruption in public procurement using data mining techniques, elements of which can be derived from ANTICORRP research. Such a system should not be deterred by the absence of procurement data, as the availability or transparency of procurement data can be built into the indicator itself and become an important weapon for both advancing transparency and grounding research.

Policy recommendations

According to ANTICORRP'S model, control of corruption in a society has thus to be understood as a complex balancing act rather than as a few separate factors determining corruption. Therefore anti-corruption (AC) cannot be effective unless it manages to assemble these features:

1. AC is adjusted to the real equilibrium level (particular transactions are either the exception or the norm) as very two different sets of policies apply (contextual);
2. if particular (corrupt) transactions are widespread AC needs to affect more than one element of the equilibrium (comprehensive);
3. if particular transactions are widespread, AC needs to be radical and strong enough to affect the balance and so trigger a disequilibrium (deep);
4. if particular transactions are widespread AC needs to involve both state (e.g. fiscal transparency) and society (watchdog NGOs) in order to influence both sides of the formula (balanced);
5. if particular transactions are widespread AC needs to result from action by those groups on all sides (state and society) who oppose the institutional status quo (genuine 'principals') and cannot be simply conceived as top-down 'reforms'.

The Bulgarian case study provides the illustration for these seemingly abstract recommendations. The lessons learnt from the Bulgarian country case study substantiate the findings that corruption is a multi-dimensional phenomenon, which is difficult to target through simple policy instruments. It demonstrates that there are many factors at play, which influence the governance regime and corrupt behaviour, and that changes are unlikely to occur in a top down fashion even under the harshest conditionality in the world, that of the European Union's Cooperation and Verification Mechanism. The case study suggests that improving governance further might be more difficult, requiring more time and more intensive efforts over a broad range of policies.

The report argues that after not even marginal progress was reached in areas such as effectiveness and impartiality of judiciary or e-government reforms the equilibrium can be affected by broader policy reforms which will indirectly impact corruption.

For instance, ***health and pension systems*** are currently heavily dependent on administrative and political decisions. The interests of services are not matched with contributions; as a result revenues are far behind expenses and only budget transfers keep the systems functioning and elementary subsistence level. This gives the political class leverage in times of elections and does not permit a sustainable development based on endogenous factors. Both systems (in view of people who do not contribute in full or on a regular basis) tend to generate substantial amounts of 'grey' behaviour. In this respect, in addition to other aspects, reforms should aim at matching contributions and benefits and limit discretionary power of officials and the political class. By reducing the underfunding of these systems in a transparent way corruption will be reduced. To challenge the equilibrium the authors suggest the removal of monopolistic legislation, a part of which is currently under attack at the European Court of Justice.

Similarly, the chapter on EU funds does not recommend that more procedures be introduced. Those do exist in abundance, complicating the access to these funds but not controlling corruption, as in corrupt environments they are simply not implemented. Where country specific research confirms the higher corruption risks associated with EU funds, the EU will have to consider advancing a radical change of policy for protecting its financial interests and promoting good governance, such as **the reallocation of EU funding going into discretionary investment projects, which typically constitute high corruption risks, towards non-discretionary spending such as unemployment benefit or another form of universalistic distribution which excludes or minimizes discretionary allocation.**

1. Ukraine: the New Sick Country of Europe

ANDREW WILSON

The Ukrainian Uprising in February 2014 was both caused by, and helped reveal, the extent of corruption in the country. Estimates are now that President Yanukovych and his circle stole $100 billion in just under four years. Ukraine has always been a badly-governed neo-patrimonial state; corruption has been endemic since independence in 1991. It now faces a huge task to put its house in order, as Russia claims it is basically a 'failed state'.

George Soros is credited with saying 'Ukraine gives corruption a bad name'. After the bloody uprising in Kyiv in February 2014 and the flight of President Yanukovych, Ukrainian prosecutors estimated the total amount of graft by Yanukovych and his literal and metaphorical 'family' at $100 billion in just short of four years. Yanukovych took $32 billion to Russia with him, much of it literally crossing the border in trucks (Falconbridge, Dabrowska and Grey 2014). The latter claim seems initially physically impossible, but whole convoys were reported. The general sum also seems beyond belief; it amounts to $25 billion a year when Ukraine's total GDP was around $180 billion. But there is detailed evidence from particular sectors that, if properly investigated (which was not the case after Ukraine's 'Orange Revolution' in 2004), may in time show how the total level of corruption added up. So pervasive was corruption, that the same prosecutors have also started investigating massive fraud in the construction of their new offices in central Kyiv.

1. Ukraine's economic structure: the roots of corruption

Ukraine's economic structure has long been both a source of corruption and a barrier to democratisation. Ukraine does not have a full-blown 'resource curse', where abundant energy or raw materials turn local politics into cut-throat rent-seeking competition, and in some states allow a generous social contract to limit the demand for democracy. Ukraine is not an energy state like Russia, but it does have a 'rentier curse'. Oligarchs and politicians, who are often enough one and the same, have been able to extract rents from metals and minerals and from Ukraine's role as an energy transit state. But they have proved unable to develop the economy. From the very onset of its transition the Ukrainian power brokers tried to control, rather than unleash economic competition, as they were seeking to secure their rents more than to achieve a successful transformation (Åslund 2009; Mungiu-Pippidi 2010; EBRD 2013). This approach kept the spoils enough to make some oligarchs rich, but not the people.

Gas is at the heart of the problem: according to a famous saying attributed to one Ukrainian oligarch Ihor Bakai in the 1990s, 'all rich people in Ukraine made their money on Russian gas'. According to another popular metaphor, gas is to Ukraine like cocaine was to Colombia. Until the Orange Revolution in 2004, Ukraine received massively subsidised Russian and Central Asian gas at $50 per 1,000 m^3, when its average level of imports was 60 billion m^3 per annum (Ukrainian heavy industry is hugely energy-inefficient). In January 2006 Russia engineered a gas cut-off to punish the leaders of the Orange Revolution, and the price was controversially forced up to $230, though mixed with Central Asian gas discounted to $95 in a corrupt scheme involving RosUkrEnergo (see below). Only in 2009 did Ukraine agree to market prices, after another cut-off in the depth of winter, with the price rapidly topping $400. From 1991 to 2009 therefore a massive gas subsidy was corruptly divided between Ukrainian and Russian politicians, at the expense of taxpayers in both states. Businesses still divert huge amounts of gas that is nominally supplied to households at a quarter of the import price (Ukrainian households supposedly consume two and a half times more gas than their richer Polish equivalents). Ukrainian companies like Oil and Gas of Ukraine have therefore built up huge debts, also because oligarchs used them for slush funds and covert funding of political projects.

Cheap gas has also inflated the profit margins of raw material (iron ore, one quarter of the world's manganese, mercury and titanium) and metals oligarchs, who sell half of Ukraine's total exports. Giant oligarch-controlled steel and chemical companies in east Ukraine also depend for their profitability on artificially cheap inputs from coking and electricity firms, whose losses are covered by the state. Alternatively, coal supplied by oligarchs was bought at artificially high prices by regional energy distributors when they were controlled by the state. Ultimately, the taxpayer again pays the burden of all these schemes, growth is artificially depressed and the Ukrainian economy has consistently under-performed.

In policy terms, Ukraine also got off on the wrong track more or less immediately after 1991. Its early economic priority was not building a market economy but recreating a mini Soviet Union, rebuilding on a local level the system of controls and extractive institutions that soon fell victim to state capture by vested interests. Controlled prices and a thicket of subsidies and monopoly privileges created a dream environment for arbitrage and rip-off merchants (Åslund 2009, pp. 55-6). Many of Ukraine's early 'oligarchs' in the 1990s were pure traders and speculators. Others made money on gas. In the late 1990s and 2000s a new generation of oligarchs emerged, largely based in the steel industry, whose wealth depended on a supply of cheap inputs (coal, electricity), corruptly off-loaded onto loss-making state institutions. Both Ukraine's oligarchs and the state bureaucracy are also parasitic on the massive but insecure shadow economy, which various estimates put as high as 40% or more of GDP (Sutela 2012). Over-regulation and over-taxation has seen Ukraine slide down the global Ease of Doing Business Scale, from 128th in 2006 to 145th in 2011 and 152nd in 2012 (Ease of Doing Business in Ukraine).

Longer-term trends may undermine this pattern of rent-seeking. 80% of Russian gas to Europe used to be routed though Ukraine. The alternative Nord Stream pipeline via the Baltic Sea started operating in 2011 and could bypass the Ukrainian system in tandem with the less certain South Stream project. By 2012 Ukraine was being forced to explore its shale gas and liquefied natural gas options, though this could be a mixed blessing if it made the local oligarchs even stronger still.

Because of bad policy and the burden of rent-seeking, Ukraine's economy has consistently under-performed. Twice it has had to be brought back from the brink, with reform periods in 1994-5 and 2000-01 that did just enough to stabilise the situation, but no more, until in both cases further reform was derailed by the oligarchs. Ukraine has extensive private ownership, but the method of sale used was corrupt and the end result insecure. Ukraine passed privatisation laws as early as 1992, but did not implement them. Voucher privatisation in 1995-7 was a dead end. Most big enterprises were then sold by discount cash sales under President Leonid Kuchma (served 1994-2005). This converted the commodity traders and 'red directors' (bosses of former communist enterprises) into a new class of 'oligarchs'. Their defenders argue that they bought their businesses at close to fair value and then grew their profits. But most sales were under highly restrictive rules, Ukraine's favourite method being elaborate legal definition of who might qualify as a bidder. The most notorious example was the sale of the steel mill Kryvorizhstal to the two main oligarchs for $800 million to ensure their support in the 2004 election. It was subsequently nationalised and resold for $4.8 billion after the election.

But without an effective and politically autonomous legal system, violent corporate raiding was widespread. The line between an oligarchic and a mafia economy remains thin, and the oligarchs still frequently quarrel among themselves; but are usually restrained by their sense of common interest, coming closest to a split in 2004, but not close enough. In three regions where the state had least control - Crimea, the Donbas and Odesa - violent mafia wars marred the 1990s as various groups struggled for control of protection and smuggling rackets.

2. The Yushchenko regime

Despite the promise of the Orange Revolution, corruption continued once Viktor Yushchenko was President from January 2005. In some ways it was worse – it was less regulated than under Kuchma, and constant political infighting meant that patron-client relations were fluid and there was less agreement on what was permissible.

Not only was there no real attempt to root out corruption in the energy sector, it became the main factor corrupting the incoming authorities. Most notorious was the transit company RosUkrEnergo, set up under Kuchma in 2004, but which was now directly offered by the Russians to circles close to Yushchenko, including his older brother.

The Ukrainian share of RosUkrEnergo ('Ros' stands for Russia, 'Ukr' for Ukraine) was $500 million a quarter, or $2 billion a year.[1] The scheme's origins dated back to Ukrainian oligarch Dmytro Firtash, who admitted his links to mobster Semion Mogilevich in a 2008 Wikileaks cable[2]. Firtash was arrested in Austria in 2014. The

---
[1] Author's interview with Oleh Rybachuk, Yushchenko's then Chief of Staff, 16 May 2013.
[2] See Wikileaks (n.d) The Public Library of US diplomacy. Ukraine: Firtash makes his Case to the USG; http://www.wikileaks.org/plusd/cables/08KYIV2414_a.html.

scheme also led to poisonous infighting within the 'Orange' governments after 2005, and helped link Yushchenko to his theoretical opposites in the Party of Regions who controlled the Prime Minister's office and government in 2006-07: Firtash, Yanukovych, his future chief of staff Serhiy Liovochkin and Energy Minister Yuriy Boyko (Global Witness 2006). The same people were back in power after 2010.

3. The Yanukovych era

The election of Viktor Yanukovych as Ukrainian President took corruption to another level. Initially, like Kuchma, he had to balance the oligarchs. But Yanukovych was a leading member of the group that emerged victorious from the Donbas gang wars of the 1990s, who were not used to sharing anything. One by one, the circle of favoured oligarchs narrowed and power became increasingly concentrated in the hands of Yanukovych's literal and metaphorical 'family', most notably his elder son Oleksandr Yanukovych and his associates like Serhiy Kurchenko. Political power was ruthlessly centralised and so was corruption, which, once it was increasingly monopolised by the 'Family', exploded in scale. When the Maidan protests against Yanukovych were just beginning in November 2013 (actually sparked by the decision to abandon a key trade deal with the EU, but against the venality and brutality of the regime in general), Anders Åslund estimated the level of corruption at $8 billion to $10 billion a year to the Yanukovych 'family' (Åslund 2013). But once the protestors were victorious and Yanukovych fled, more information became available. When Arseniy Yatseniuk took over as Prime Minister, he initially claimed: '37 billion dollars of credit received have disappeared in an unknown direction... (and) the sum of 70 billion dollars was paid out of Ukraine's financial system into off-shore accounts' (Balmforth 2014). For perspective, $70 billion was equivalent to almost half Ukraine's gross domestic product in 2013. Only 4.3 billion UAH (Ukrainian Hryvnia, or $430 million) was left in government accounts, Yatseniuk said, and only $15 billion in the central bank's foreign currency reserves. Within two months, the estimate of total corruption had risen to $100 billion. Prosecutors and civil society were also able to give a better account of how corruption worked under Yanukovych.

Gas was still the biggest area of 'traditional' corruption. The notorious RosUkrEnergo had lost its position in 2009, but a gas price discount agreed by Russia in 2010 actually made the situation worse, increasing the scope for arbitrage.

A massive 7.5% of GDP went on energy subsidies, of which 2% of GDP was to the state oil and gas company Naftohaz Ukraïny. Åslund describes how Naftohaz bought 18 billion m^3 of domestically produced gas per year at the extremely low price $53 per 1000 m^3, because it was supposed to supply hard-pressed domestic consumers. However, at least half of that gas found its way to industrial customers or straight to the companies of favoured oligarchs, or went abroad for a price nearer the then Russian supply price of $410 per 1000 m^3. As Åslund notes, 'the potential for privileged arbitrage here is enormous: $350 per 1000 m^3 times 9 billion m^3 equals $3.15 billion. This is probably the main reason why Yanukovych so adamantly opposes increased gas prices' (Åslund

2013). An investigation by slidstvo.info shows how 'Yanukovych's gas kings' divided up the domestic market (Slidstvo.info).

Insider privatisations were the key means of initially keeping non-Family oligarchs happy in 2010-11. Rinat Akhmetov in particular was able to add regional power companies to his empire. Dmytro Firtash won control of the local fertiliser industry. Nobody knows who bought the majority stake in Ukrtelecom in 2010 (Matuszak 2012). But by 2012 the regime was running out of further assets to disburse.

State procurement was the biggest area of new corruption. Once physical assets threatened to run out, corruption was increasingly concentrated on the state budget. 'Over-payment was everywhere, in every ministry'.[3] Kurchenko was responsible for organising the pyramid and collecting the money up, also with Artem Pshonka, the General Prosecutor's son. The chain led back to Yanukovych. 'He was the father, he could do anything'. The 'cut was maybe 10% under Kuchma, but 50% under Lazarenko. Under Yanukovych it could be even higher'.[4]

The public procurement law passed in June 2010 was soon being undermined by all sorts of loopholes; in July 2012 all state-owned companies were exempted from open tender (See ANTAC website: http://antac.org.ua). The amount of unmonitored, basically secret, procurement then simply exploded: it was 250 billion UAH in the next twelve months ($21.1 billion) (Nikolov and Shalaisky 2012).

Serhiy Kurchenko was key to the procurement scams. His chain of influence was made up of hundreds of fake Ukrainian companies and dozens of offshore firms, which worked on the principle of terrorist cells, divided into small groups who were not allowed to talk to each other (Babinets 2014).

'The same firms kept taking part in tenders conducted by one of the subsidiaries of the Ministry of Energy and Coal. Billions were taken from the budget by these firms, even though they had nothing to do with these works and equipment. They exaggerated purchase prices by sixty times or more. Then they appropriated these funds through fictitious companies. The same situation existed in the Ministry of Taxes' (Mahnitsky 2014). The former head of the department organised a number of front companies to minimize tax liabilities, leading to tax evasion amounting to over 6 billion UAH ($508 million) (*ibid*). Procurement also worked backwards, for money laundering and theft of state funds.

4. Euro-2012

Another reason why procurement corruption took off in 2012 was that Ukraine had won the right to co-host the finals of the European Football Championship with Poland. Corruption in the Euro 2012 building process meant rake-offs of more than a third on most projects, especially after the incoming Yanukovych administration abolished competitive tendering for most contracts in 2010 (Franchetti and Jaber

---

[3] Interview with Daria Kaleniuk, Executive Director of Ukraine's Anti-Corruption Action Centre, http://antac.org.ua, 9 June 2014.
[4] *ibid.*

2012). The Summer Olympics in London in 2012 over-ran their original budget of £9.3 billion ($15.8 billion). But the Ukrainians spent quite a bit, and they were only co-hosts. One investigation claimed a total cost of $14 billion (Matlack 2012); The Economist estimated $13 billion (2012), but nobody really knows how much.

Ukraine concentrated on mega-projects. Four shining new stadia went up in the host cities of Kyiv, Lviv, Kharkiv and Donetsk. Kyiv's new Olympic stadium cost an estimated $600 million, half as much again as the Allianz Arena in Munich that was built for the World Cup finals in Germany in 2006. Infrastructure upgrades have concentrated on airports, which is sensible enough for Ukraine's long-term business future, but ordinary Ukrainians did not see the benefit.

5. Phantom companies

Scam procurement payments were often channelled through another favourite scam using companies that disappeared immediately after payments were made or simply never existed at all. These 'phantom firms [were] suspected of squeezing a total of 130 billion UAH ($11 billion) from Kyiv's coffers over the past three years', at a time when 'the country's total tax revenue amounted to 210 billion UAH ($17.8 billion) in 2013' (Danilova and Slatter 2014). The way that the scam often worked was that state agencies pretended to buy goods or services from the phantom firm but instead of delivering on the deal, the fake company secretly returned the money in cash, reducing the real company's tax liability in return for a cut of the money. The tax boss Oleksandr Klymenko ran one of the schemes himself. 'Klymenko had a vault was equipped with a white-noise generator to beat eavesdroppers and furnished with clear plastic tables and chairs so those haggling over their spoils could see there were no listening devices attached to the furniture' (*ibid*).

Fake Bankruptcies were another popular scheme. State-owned companies would overspend, or fail to deliver product. They would then say they could not cover their bills and take a loan from a 'family' bank. Then they would file for bankruptcy and the loan would disappear as the insolvency process was corruptly managed. The bank would then take over the company at penny cost – a form of privatisation without payment.

Another similar scheme involved forcing firms to pay into such schemes or over-pay into oligarchs' own firms. For example the oligarch who dominated Luhansk oblast in the east Oleksandr Yefremov, forced the local Stakhanov ferroalloy plant to purchase gas at two or three times the normal price to drive it under.

VAT refunds have long been a problem in Ukraine. Companies had to pay bribes to move up the queue, or simply to get the refund at all. In the 2000s they developed into a form of collusive corruption: companies would put in inflated claims and pay a commission on the refund, increasingly through shadowy intermediary companies, dubbed *firmy-prokladky*, meaning 'padding firms'. Once again, under Yanukovych this process was monopolised, and all organised under only one permissible channel. The payment to these types of companies was given the local euphemism of 'information services'.

Serhiy Kurchenko also specialised in evading customs. His VETEK group of companies and subsidiaries imported 25 billion UAH ($2.1 billion) worth of oil in 2012-13 for refining, but pretended to re-export it, which allowed the company to avoid massive tax payments. The products were then sold in Ukraine though a chain of fictitious firms. Everyone had to buy from him.

Illegal coal mines, or *copanky*, have existed in Ukraine for more than two decades. Originally, they were a means for the local poor to try and scrape a dangerous living, but as soon as they showed signs of making reasonable money they came under the influence of organised crime and afterwards by 'businessmen' backed by state officials. Private companies were buying coal from up to 2,500 *copanky*, processing it and selling it as if they had mined it by themselves.

Once again, starting from 2010 the process was monopolised, in this case by the President's older son Oleksandr Yanukovych. In 2012 6.5 million tons of coal was mined illegally. Coincidentally, Yanukovych's MAKO company sold 6.65 million tons (Savitsky 2013), mainly to the two local state-owned electricity providers, Donbasenergo and Tsentrenergo, which in the six months over the winter of 2012-13 bought 12 billion UAH worth of coal ($1 billion) from companies close to Oleksandr Yanukovych's circle (Gumenyuk, Gobert and Geslin 2013).

Coal miners' trade unions estimated that if the annual amount was around 6 to 7 million tons, and with an average price for coal of about $100 per ton, the annual output of illegally mined coal could be worth $700 million. The Yanukovych regime robbed their home region as enthusiastically as they robbed the government in Kyiv.

6. Raiderstvo

Ukraine under Yanukovych also saw an explosion of simple extortion. According to the Federation of Employers of Ukraine (UNIAN 2014), the amount of bribes Ukrainian business had to pay officials reached 160 billion UAH per year ($13.5 billion), mainly direct bribes and kickbacks paid during the procurement procedure, the return of VAT, customs and relations in agriculture.

So-called *raiderstvo* was a world away from commercial raiding in the West. It meant the takeover of companies through violence or the threat of violence, or undermining them with kompromat and legal cases.

Raiderstvo was not challenged but promoted by the law. One of the many functions of the destruction of courts' independence by the 2010 'legal reform' (in fact an imposition of executive control over the judiciary) was to *monopolise* corruption and to use the courts for the legalisation, if not the legitimation, of *raiderstvo*.

The General Prosecutors Office 'had a special office to monitor the most profitable businesses.' Any sign of financial health would trigger proceedings, inspections, etc. In the 'light version' bribes had to be paid to survive. In the 'heavy version' owners would actually be imprisoned.[5] It would be hard to think of any action more inimical to economic growth.

---

[5] *ibid.*

Conclusion

The evidence found at Mezhyhirya and elsewhere was both damming and colourful. Among the documents found after Yanukovych's flight were a '$12 million handwritten cheque to an undisclosed beneficiary, a €39 million chandelier supply contract' (Luxmoore 2014). The evidence also uncovered the lifestyle of the President's inner circle, the privileged twenty-eight who belonged to his hunting club (Akimenko, Babinets and Sedletska 2014), which ultimately helps explain why their behaviour was self-defeating. The 'Family' was too greedy and too destructive. Their schemes drove the Ukrainian economy into the ground. But 'they lived in another reality. They didn't know when to stop.'[6] The challenge for Ukraine is now the same as after the Orange Revolution – how not to miss the creation of an open order access so that after pushing down a neo-patrimonial regime they settle for a regime of competitive clientelism (North, Wallis and Weingast 2009; Mungiu-Pippidi 2006). In other words, Ukraine is the chief case of limited access order in Europe, and the EU does not have much experience in changing such regimes. Italy and Greece are living proof how difficult governance is to change even under beneficial external influence – and Ukraine is subject to conflicting influences and other major threats.

References

Anticorruption Action Centre (n.d.) *Advocacy*. Available from: <http://antac.org.ua/en/advocating/>

Åslund, A. (2009) How Ukraine Became a Market Economy and Democracy, (Washington, DC: Peterson Institute), pp. 55-6

Åslund, A. (2013) 'Payback time for the "Yanukovych Family"', 11 December 2013. Available from: <http://blogs.piie.com/realtime/?p=4162>

Akimenko, O., Babinets, A. and Sedletska, N. (2014) '28 Friends of the President', *Yanukovych Leaks*, 26 April 2014. Available from: <http://stories.yanukovychleaks.org/28-friends-of-the-president/>

Babinets, A. (2014) 'How Kurchenko's offshores worked', *Yanukovych Leaks*, 6 April 2014. Available from: <http://stories.yanukovychleaks.org/how-kurchenkos-offshores-worked/>

Balmforth, R. (2014) 'Billions received by Yanukovich [sic] government have disappeared: PM Yatseniuk', *Reuters*, 27 February 2014. Available from: <www.reuters.com/article/2014/02/27/us-ukraine-crisis-money-idUSBREA1Q14Q20140227>

Danilova, M. and Slatter, D. (2014) 'Nationwide Pyramid Scheme Run by a Yanukovych Crony Squeezed $11 Billion from Ukraine', *The Business Insider*, 10 June 2014. Available from: <http://www.businessinsider.com/pyramid-scheme-run-by-yanukovych-ally-2014-6>

European Bank for Reconstruction and Development (EBRD) (2013) *Stuck in Transition*. Available from: <http://www.ebrd.com/downloads/research/transition/tr13.pdf>

Faulconbridge, G., Dabrowska, A. and Grey, S. (2014) 'Toppled "mafia" president cost Ukraine up to $100 billion, prosecutor says', *Reuters*, 30 April 2014. Available from: <www.reuters.com/article/2014/04/30/us-ukraine-crisis-yanukovich-idUSBREA3T0K820140430>

Franchetti, M. and Jaber, H. (2012) 'Ukraine leader's cronies "grab cash meant for Euro 2012"', *The Sunday Times*, 3 June 2012. Available from: < http://www.thesundaytimes.co.uk/sto/news/world_news/Europe/article1051983.ece>

---

[6] *ibid.*

Global Witness (2006) *It's a Gas. Funny Business in the Turkmen-Ukraine Gas Trade*, 25 July 2006. Available from: <www.globalwitness.org/library/its-gas-funny-business-turkmen-ukraine-gas-trade>

Golovnev, S. (2014) 'This is how makeshift coalmine business is arranged in Ukraine', 22 January 2014, translated from *Forbes*, 27 May 2013. Available from: <http://antac.org.ua/en/2014/01/this-is-how-makeshift-coalmine-business-is-arranged-in-ukraine/>

Gumenyuk, N., Gobert, S. and Geslin, L. (2013) 'Digging for Billions', *The Ukrainian Week*, 15 March 2013. Available from: <http://ukrainianweek.com/Society/74747>

International Finance Corporation (n.d.) 'Ease of Doing Business in Ukraine'. Available from: <http://www.doingbusiness.org/data/exploreeconomies/ukraine/>

Luxmoore, M. (2014) 'Journalists gather for Mezhyhirya Fest investigative conference at fugitive ex-president's estate', *The Kyiv Post*, 8 June 2014. Available from: <www.kyivpost.com/content/ukraine/journalists-gather-for-mezhyhirya-fest-investigative-conference-at-fugitive-ex-presidents-estate-351131.html>

Matlack, C. (2012) 'Poland, Ukraine suffer as Euro soccer hosts', *Bloomberg Business Week*, 8 June 2012. Available from: <www.businessweek.com/articles/2012-06-08/poland-ukraine-suffer-as-euro-soccer-hosts>

Matuszak, S. (2012) 'The Oligarchic Democracy. The Influence of Business Groups on Ukrainian Politics', *OSW Studies*, No. 42, September 2012. Available from: <www.osw.waw.pl/sites/default/files/prace_42_en.pdf>

Mungiu-Pippidi, A. (2006) 'Corruption: Diagnosis and Treatment', *Journal of Democracy*, July 2006, Vol. 17, No. 3, pp. 86-99

Mungiu-Pippidi, A. (2010) 'Twenty Years of Postcommunism: The Other Transition', *Journal of Democracy*, January 2010, Vol. 21, No. 1, pp. 120-27

Nikolov, Y. and Shalaiskii, A. (2012) 'Tenders in Ukraine. Eyes Wide Shut', *Dzerkalo tyzhnia*, 17 February 2012. Available from: <http://gazeta.zn.ua/POLITICS/tendery_v_ukraine__s_shiroko_zakrytymi_glazami.html>

North, D., Wallis J.J. and Weingast B.R. (2009) *Violence and Social Orders: A Conceptual Framework for Interpreting Recorded Human History*. New York: Cambridge University Press

Savitsky, O. (2013) 'Yanukovich [sic] regime earns billions on illegal coal mining'. Available from: <http://350.org/yanukovich-regime-earns-billions-on-illegal-coal-mining>

Slidstvo (2012) 'Kings Ukrainian Gas (Koroliukraïns'kohohazu - 2)', 17 August 2012. Available from: <http://slidstvo.info/rozsliduvannia/5-2.html>

Sutela, P. (2012) 'The Underachiever: Ukraine's Economy Since 1991', *Carnegie Endowment for International Peace* March 2012. Available from: <http://carnegieendowment.org/2012/03/09/underachiever-ukraine-s-economy-since-1991>

The Economist (2012) 'The best tournament money can buy', 29 May 2012. Available from: <www.economist.com/blogs/easternapproaches/2012/05/ukraine-and-euro-2012>

UNIAN (2014) 'Yanukovych's Circle Illegally Took around $100 Billion Over the Border', 19 May 2014. Available from: <http://economics.unian.ua/finance/919570-otochennya-yanukovicha-nezakonno-vivelo-za-kordon-blizko-100-mlrd.html>

Prosecutor General of Ukraine (2014) 'Due to corruption schemes in the sphere of state procurement the state lost billions of hryvnia - Oleg Mahnitsky', 3 June 2014. Available from: <www.gp.gov.ua/ua/news.html?_m=publications&_t=rec&id=139434&fp=10>

Wikileaks (n.d) 'Ukraine: Firtash makes his Case to the USG', *The Public Library of US diplomacy*. 10 Dec 2008. Available from: <http://www.wikileaks.org/plusd/cables/ 08KYIV2414_a.html>

2. Bulgarian Anti-Corruption Reforms: a Lost Decade?

ALEXANDER STOYANOV, RUSLAN STEFANOV AND BORYANA VELCHEVA

Why are Bulgarians protesting in the streets against corruption and voting out government after government despite so many reforms inspired by the EU? This chapter argues that corruption is a key element to understand the Bulgarian governance regime, i.e. the way political and administrative power are acquired, used, structured, delegated and reproduced. Currently the governance regime of Bulgaria can best be described as having moved gradually from patrimonialism towards open access order, but most of its features are still in the competitive particularism stage when various power factions compete for spoils (Mungiu-Pipiddi et al. 2011). Bulgarian governance has progressed since 1998 in particular as related to administrative (petty) corruption, but it is has not yet evolved into an open access order.

The dynamics of corruption victimisation as measured by Center for the Study of Democracy, leads to the conclusion that the main change occurred in the beginning of the 2000s, which resulted in the lowest levels of administrative corruption reached in 2004. These were two times lower than in 1998. Since 2004 change has become more gradual and uneven with some regress immediately after the country's EU accession (CSD 2013a). It seems probable that the country will continue to experience decreasing levels of administrative corruption. However, overcoming higher-level, political corruption is unlikely to happen in the foreseeable future. It will require action on the part of the judiciary and further external pressure coming from the EU (European Commission 2014).

The main trends in governance regime transformation in Bulgaria can be traced by the reaction of politicians from the respective incumbent governments to the rising tide of corruption surveys and reports after 1997. Following EU accession in 2007, the anti-corruption drive weakened and even reversed, widening the implementation gap between existing regulations and actual results. This clashed with rising expectations for more transparency and universalism on the part of civil society and the EC, culminating in financial sanctions from the EC (EU funds for Bulgaria were suspended in 2008) and blocking of the country's further EU integration (e.g. Bulgaria has not been allowed to become a member of the border free Schengen area, or the Eurozone), as well as in citizen street protests in 2013-14.

In its latest report on Bulgaria under the Cooperation and Verification Mechanism the European Commission notes, that 'overall progress has been not yet sufficient and fragile' (European Commission 2014, p. 9). It can thus be concluded that according to the EC in the 15 years after it began EU accession talks with Bulgaria in 1999 the country has not made sufficient progress to become a full-fledged EU member. Most international indicators confirm the EC's findings on Bulgaria in relation to good governance and corruption. According to the Worldwide Governance Indicators (Kaufman, Kraay and Mastruzzi 2013) Bulgaria made good progress in the Control of Corruption dimension in the period 1996–2003 but then stagnated in what might seem a lost decade (**Figure 1**).

Transparency International's Corruption Perception Index (CPI) reveals a similar dynamic with Bulgarian's perception of corruption improving between 1998 and 2002, then stagnating for four years, only to worsen after the country's EU accession, reaching its lowest value in 2011[1]. The Global Integrity Report (2010) showed that Bulgaria faced a large implementation gap in relation to its anti-corruption legislation.

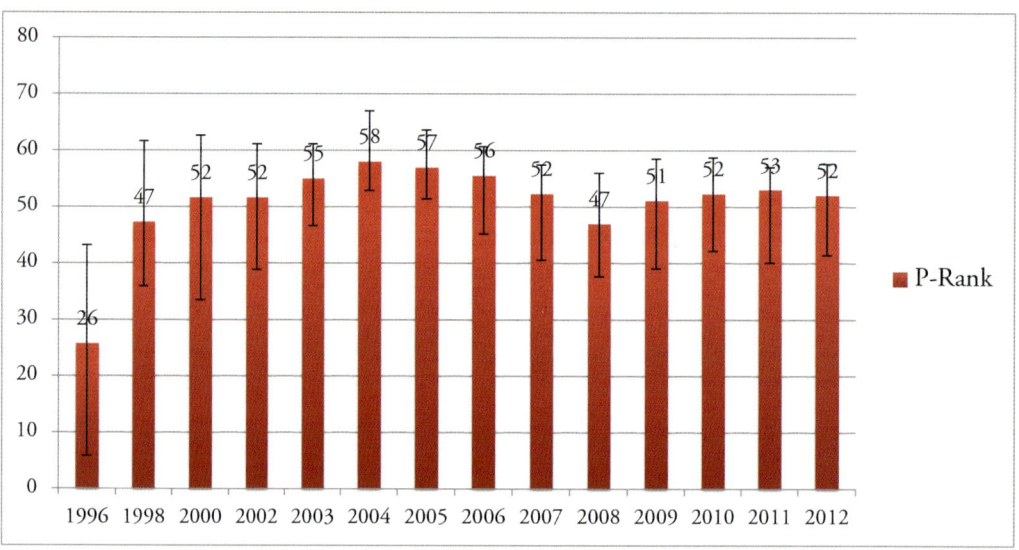

Figure 1. Bulgaria's percentile rank (p-rank) in the control of corruption dimension of the Worldwide Governance Indicators (1996 – 2012).

Note: P-Rank denotes Bulgaria's percentile rank among all countries (ranges from 0 (lowest) to 100 (highest) rank). The error-bars mark the upper and lower bound of the of 90% confidence interval for governance, in percentile rank terms
Source: Kaufman, Kraay and Mastruzzi 2013.

1. Mechanisms of transformation

There have been many factors at play, shaping the current state of the governance regime in Bulgaria, which can be clustered in two groups. On the one hand - the downside, public services in Bulgaria have been chronically underfunded, corruption and informality have been largely accepted as a norm of social behaviour, power was concentrated in the hands of a very limited number of communist era apparatchiks,

---

[1] Transparency International changed the methodology of calculating the country CPI scores in 2012, which rendered comparisons to previous years impossible, but Bulgaria remained ranked in the 70th percentile, showing no real progress in anti-corruption.

which became the godfathers of Bulgarian democracy and market economy, and the country's formal institutions for identifying, prosecuting and punishing corrupt behaviour have been weak and unprepared for acting in a globalised economy and liberalised political system. On the other hand – the upside, Bulgaria has become a member of the EU, which has been monitoring the country's progress in the area of anti-corruption and judicial reform, modern technologies and formal institutions introduced through the country's EU membership have created and gradually increased demand for accountability and rule of law.

A substantial corruption generation factor (still not acknowledged by most policy makers) is the lack of balance of interests in the construction of many important social systems. For example, although health care and the pension system are in principle fund based, the individual contributions to the system are not linked to the services provided. Reports show that more than 1 million Bulgarians (out of a population of 7.3 million) do not pay health insurance (Pashev 2007). Pensions received are more dependent on political decisions than individual contributions; hence there is an inbuilt interest to bypass income declaration legislation and receive 'grey incomes'. The policies employed to deal with these corruption generators (higher sanctions and more administrative control[2]) generate even more corruption (Nonchev et al. 2011).

Political response to corruption in Bulgaria has been specific and reflects the structured link between the business sector, the judiciary and the political class. All parties have been collecting information about abuses of those in power. However, this has not been used to initiate prosecution, forced resignations, etc., but as a 'background tool' to threaten the opponent and to use in political negotiations. This 'omerta' explains why practically no (with very few minor exceptions) high-level members of the ruling elite (past and current) have been accused and/or sentenced on corruption charges. In recent years it has become quite common to accuse the previous members of the executive of abuse of power, start prosecution and then drop all charges (due to lack of enough evidence). Bulgarian politicians have routinely responded to external pressure to deliver results in fighting corruption by focusing on low-level administrative corruption in the form of bribery. As a result, there has been a gradual increase in the number of convicted individuals for bribery, at the expense of convictions for more complex corruption crimes such as abuse of office (or malfeasance).

1.1 Power distribution

Although there is increasing political competition, power remains concentrated in party political leaders, with strong influence from business interests, which has led to recurring conflicts of interest, loss of popular trust in institutions and parties, and the emergence and disappearing of many political players. Since the democratic changes in the country in 1989 and the first free elections in the most recent history of the

---

[2] The most common policy construction 'mantra' is that more government agencies, more control and higher sanctions will effectively counter anti-systemic and corruption behavior. This is closely linked to the perception that all deviations exist because of missing legislation and lack of government control.

country in 1990, two phases of power distribution can be differentiated. The first phase (1990-2001) was characterized by the polarized battle between the numerous newly formed opposition parties, united in the Union of Democratic Forces (UDF), and the transformed Bulgarian Communist Party, which changed its name to the Bulgarian Socialist Party (BSP). The third big party, which emerged during the first stage of political transition, was the Movement for Rights and Freedoms (MRF), a closed, leader-centred party, representing mainly the ethnic Turks. During this period, BSP and UDF took turns in the control of legislative and executive power. But in effect the former communist party remained largely in control until 1997, successfully transforming their political into economic power.

The financial meltdown of 1996-97 gave the opposition UDF an absolute majority in power (both president and prime-minister) with a very strong mandate for reform. Under heavy conditionality imposed by the International Monetary Fund, the country went through a fire privatisation and painful public service reform. Privatisation created huge rent-seeking opportunities and was perceived by experts and the general public as a corruption-infested process, from which only politically connected people benefited. This resulted in strong disappointment and the ousting of the UDF government in 2001. The second phase of the transition period (2001–present) has been characterized by strategic and macroeconomic stability along with the emergence and decline of many parties and party opportunism.

The continuing disappointment of the Bulgarian voters with the political establishment and its inability to deal decisively with corruption led to the gradual decline of trust in the political system as evidenced by the decreasing voter turnout in general elections (**Figure 2**) and the frequent emergence and decline of new political projects and the emergence of many parties.

Figure 2. Voter turnout at national elections in Bulgaria (1991 – 2013).

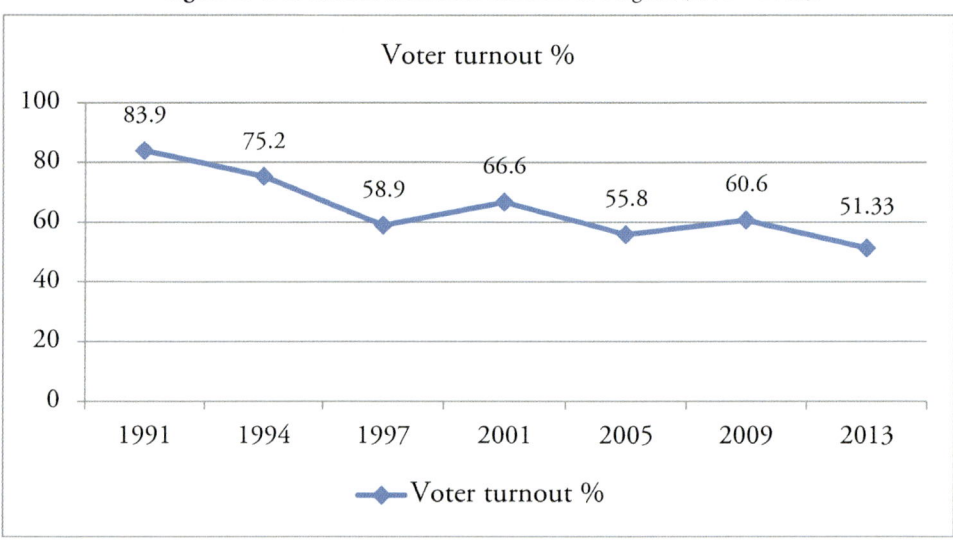

Source: Eurostat, Central Election Commission (CEC).

1.2. Consolidation of political and economic power

Falling voter turnout and the existence of parliamentary elections has benefited parties with stable electorates, such as MRF and BSP, and has made possible the emergence of political - business joint ventures of oligarchs and political engineers. These have also been lured by the sizable increase in state subsidies for political parties in 2009. At the last parliamentary elections only 4 out of the participating 36 parties and coalitions in the parliamentary elections made it past the electoral threshold of 4% of the votes, leaving a large number of voters unrepresented in the Bulgarian parliament (**Table 1**).

The system of party financing was introduced in the early 2000s to counter a rising tide of business money entering the political system during the previous decade. This phenomenon, known as 'political investment' is related to the figure of 'business politicians' described by della Porta, Rizzorno and Donaldson (1996). It developed as the most widespread type of political corruption in the country in the past two decades. In return, politicians helped 'political investors' privatize the big state-owned enterprises, thus building the future structure of large business in Bulgaria. Political investors sought access to the rising pot of resources at the disposal of the Bulgarian government, including to EU funds after the country's accession in 2007. However, 'political investment' grew more costly and thus accessible only to bigger entrepreneurs and fewer political figures. The role of the political elite and the public administration in the process increased (CSD 2009, pp. 46-54). This trend has been strengthened by the economic stagnation in Bulgaria since 2008.

Table 1. Number of political parties participating in parliamentary elections 1991-2013.

	General Election Year						
	1991	1994	1997	2001	2005	2009	2013
Total number of PP and coalitions participating in the elections	39	47	36	37	22	18	36
PP* receiving state subsidy but not elected for Parliament (i.e. received more than 1% of the votes)	4	1	1	0	2	2	6
PP and coalitions elected for Parliament (i.e. received 4% or more of the votes)	3	5	5	4	7	6	4
% of PP and coalitions, participating in the elections, which received state subsidies	17,9	12,8	16,7	10,8	40,9	44,4	27,8

* Note: Coalitions which received more than 1% but were not elected for Parliament are not eligible for state subsidy
Source: Central Election Commission (CEC), Bulgarian National Audit Office, CSD.

Due to big networks of 'political investors' the 'political weight' of a given politician became dependent not only on the political success of his or her own party, but also on their access to the largest number of entrepreneurs and networks of political investors. Parties with stable political representation (core voters) such as BSP, and in particular MRF, became more valuable as guarantors of business interests in successive parliaments. The former leader of MRF Ahmed Dogan provided a description of this ideology of networks of investors just before the parliamentary elections in 2005. He used the term 'loops of companies' to describe the fact that each political party has a network of economic groups and companies that support it financially. He also noted that no businessperson in Bulgaria has succeeded without support from political leaders. The MRF leader was then videotaped again in a public speech before the 2009 elections noting that ministers and MPs are mere figureheads and that he 'distributes the portions of power' himself (Angarev 2009).

1.3. Levels of corruption and the political establishment

The Corruption Monitoring System (CMS) developed and used by CSD since 1998 is the longest available national instrument for measuring the prevalence of corruption in Bulgaria through constructing indexes based on population and business surveys (CSD 2007). In the period between 1998 and 2013, the CMS has registered several phases in the participation of the citizens in corruption transactions which could be directly linked to the political cycle (**Figure 4**).

The first low levels of corruption were registered in 2003-04. After a rise (2005-08) new lows have been registered during the term of the CEDB government, which managed to reduce corruption pressure on the population and the business by introducing repressive, law-enforcement measures on the state administration and frequent tax inspections for businesses. The effects of the crisis, which lowered available resources for corrupt transactions, reinforced these measures. The reduction in the share of people participating in corruption has come from a decline in the pressure exerted by the public administration on the citizens.

While the active solicitation of bribes by the administration has declined, the system has remained open for corruption offers from the citizens (CSD 2013a). The share of people involved in corruption has rebounded in 2012-13 on the back of more people initiating the corruption exchange. Hence, it seems that the data suggests that a combination of more strict enforcement of integrity rules in the public administration coupled with fewer opportunities for contact between the citizens and the administration can produce lasting reduction in corruption involvement. The willingness of the people to actively engage in corruption though seems to suggest that bribe giving might have become part of the culture of communication with some parts of the public administration. The juxtaposition of the data on the level of administrative corruption in the country with the data on the control of the power reveals that unitary governments, i.e. formed by one party can lead to greater reduction in the incidence of corruption.

Figure 3. Share of the adult population who gave a bribe at least once in the last year (% of population, 18 years and older) (1999-2013).

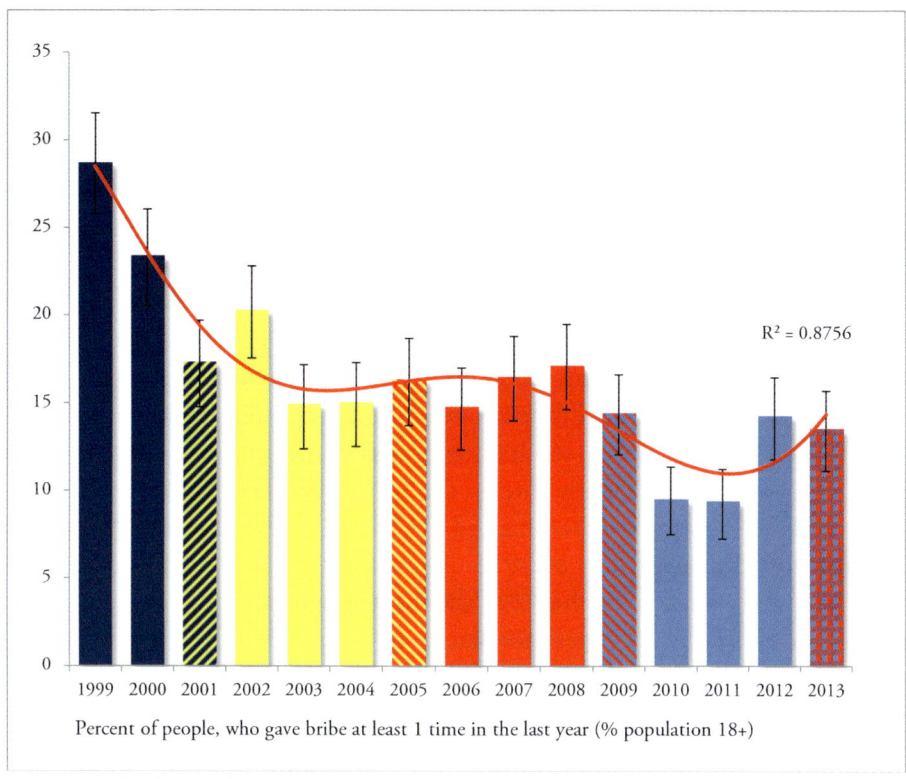

Percent of people, who gave bribe at least 1 time in the last year (% population 18+)

*Note: Data for the mandates of each government is colour-coded.
Source: CMS, CSD.

Figure 4. Share of those of the adult population who contacted the public administration who gave bribes: after pressure (i.e. on demanded from the public administration), and without pressure (i.e. no demand from the public administration) (1999 – 2013).

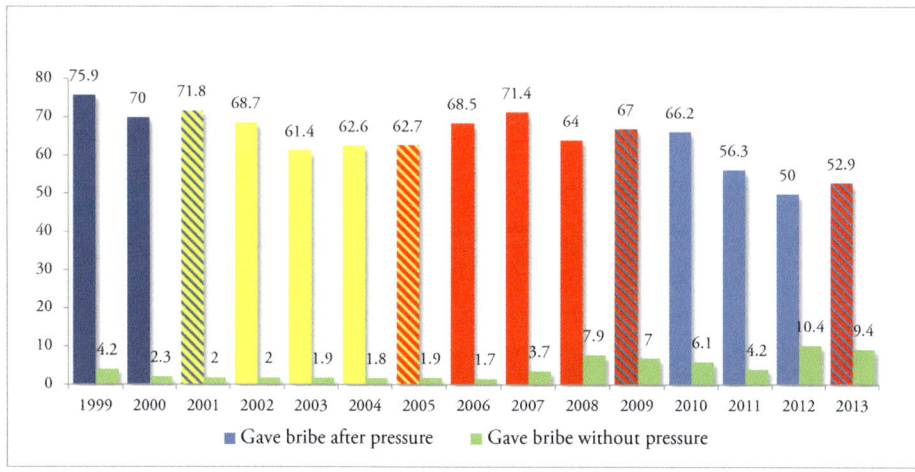

*Note: Data for the mandates of each government is colour-coded.
Source: CMS, CSD.

1.4. The roots of weak state autonomy

The autonomy of the state from private interest is low. Despite the adoption of many legal requirements for separating public from private interest, in many cases the state is captured by interest groups due to weak enforcement of rules. Changes in laws often serve particular private interests. The deep connections between state power and private interest have developed historically as a result of two processes in the beginning of the 1990's: the dismantling of the one party system, and the de-politicization of the security (including army) apparatus. These processes provoked hard political battles and continue to influence modern-day politics. Members of the former establishment continue to influence power distribution. They have created competing powerful networks, which have become independent from party and hence state, control and oversight. Often political battles revolve around competing interests and fights for control over these networks.

Bulgaria, like other Eastern European countries, and unlike old member-states is characterised by a very pervasive reach of organised crime into the formal institutions of power. This has been particularly true for the judiciary and law enforcement (Gounev and Bezlov 2012). The first ever Serious and Organised Crime Threat Assessment done for Bulgaria has revealed that as of 2011 organised crime in the country controls as much as €1.8 of revenues from the 12 of the most significant organised crime market (CSD 2012, p. 5). The assessment notes that a particularly dangerous form of organised crime -oligarchy has emerged from the fusion of violent organised crime and white collar crime when with the help of political corruption powerful economic conglomerates have been formed, which then feed on exploiting public resources through corruption and crime. These groups try to preserve their power through corrupting law enforcement, and in particular security forces and the judiciary, while incumbent politicians have tried to limit their influence through sporadic pressure through the state compliance and control bodies and/or through legislative action. The 2012 summary report of the EC under the CVM on Bulgaria's progress in the fight against corruption and organised crime during the period 2007-12 stated that the independence of the judiciary in Bulgaria remained questionable, that there were systemic failures in law enforcement and efforts to fight corruption were inhibited by the lack of independent anti-corruption institutions (European Commission 2012).

1.5. Every government appoints its own administration

Although the Act on Civil Servants (ACS), introduced in 1999, differentiates between political and professional appointments, and the courts have strengthened the independence of the public administration, a wide range of administrative positions and the local authorities are dependent on the central government. Higher-ranking administration of the most key institutions changes with each new government. This includes for example the directors of all local police departments, the management of key government agencies, such as Customs, the National Revenue Agency, the institutions of financial control, key positions in the health care and pension system (such as the director of the National Health Insurance Fund, the National Social

Security Institute), the building control agency, etc. For example, in 2013, the new Minister of Environment and Water changed the directors of all regional environmental inspection offices, the directors of the three national parks in Bulgaria and the directors of the four regional offices for water control - all of them at once (Nikolaeva 2013). The regularity of changes in all these administrative positions has allowed for the politicians in power to appoint loyal people to key positions without competitive selection, and to satisfy friendly business interests. The short and insecure terms of the administration have stalled the professionalization of the public administration allowing more private sector influence on public policy-making.

1.6. Lack of transparency in economic policies and public spending

Despite continuing improvements during the past decade, in particular after EU entry, policy-making in the country remains opaque. The link between identified socio-economic problems on the one hand, and strategy development, policy-making, budgeting and implementation, on the other hand, remains weak. EU driven national reform and convergence programmes' policy development have infused some clarity but it rarely translates into consistent policy-implementation. A particular case in point heavily affecting public spending, the flow of sizeable state resources to the private sector, and the country's economic environment have been policies and decisions on building new generation capacities in the energy sector. Despite the existence of a flat trend in electricity consumption accompanied by tripling of the country's GDP between 2001 and 2012, and despite the unrealized potential of energy efficiency gains in one of the most energy intensive economies in the EU, in the 2006-12 period, Bulgaria allowed the installation of a total of 1,563 MW of new renewable energy capacities, on top of the started project on building a 2,000 MW new nuclear power plant, the building of numerous new water power plants, and the decision to start planning the building of a new 1,000 MW reactor on the site of the existing nuclear power plant (Stefanov et al. 2011).

According to the Open Budget Index 2012, Bulgaria, with a score of 65, enjoys significant budget transparency and ranks 20th among 93 countries. Bulgaria has consistently improved its scores since 2006 when it joined the ranking but it has only managed to jump from the category of some to the category of substantial budget transparency in 2012 (IBP 2013). Since 1998 the Bulgarian government publishes monthly, quarterly and annual information on the state of implementation of the consolidated state budget, and of the government debt. However, governments have failed to report on the final actual implementation of the budget.

Although the Bulgarian government has pledged the introduction of programme budget management since 2001, it remains non-binding for the administration. For example, in 2013, the new government announced that the state budget needs to be revised only a month after taking office and without sound argumentation. The government requested and was granted by Parliament the emission of an additional debt of BGN[3] 1 billion without providing policy rationale for the spending of the newly requested resources. The budget

---

[3] BGN or Bulgarian lev. At the current exchange rate, BGN 1 = EUR 0.51

revision was rushed through parliament for less than a week, although it required two readings in the standing committees and two readings on the parliament floor.

1.7. Public procurement as a tool to provide for private interests in the government

Public services in Bulgaria are chronically underfunded, which makes the availability and quality of public goods and services poor. As such, resources are fairly centralised. The national government has strong discretionary power to distribute public goods and services to local authorities. While budget transparency provides enough data to follow up on allocations this can only happen post-factum. The national audit office has the authority to reveal waste of public resources, which it has done throughout the years but does not have any powers to prosecute.

The bad practices in public procurement in Bulgaria are so numerous that businesses and the general public persistently hold the belief that bids cannot be won without bribery and/or political protection. The most typical violation is the introduction of special requirements, which limit the possible candidates to one or maximum two (usually related) companies, one of which is the preferred winner. In order to prevent bad practices, in 2012 an electronic system of 6 components – register, bidding, catalogue, tender, monitoring and audit – was proposed. However, in its first report on the electronic system the Centre for Prevention and Countering Corruption and Organized Crime (CPCCOC) states that additional measures should be taken with regard to the normative framework, the organization and the methodology of public procurement (CPCCOC 2013, p. 22).

The volume of the government public procurement budget has declined considerably since the crisis began (**Figure 5**), limiting the opportunity for politicians and the public administration to satisfy the whole demand for public procurement, which has resulted in several very public scandals between competitors with mutual accusations of corruption practices. Some evidence from the past though has suggested that whilst growing in value, the public procurement market is shrinking in terms of number of participants, which is an indication of the concentration of public resources channelled to private operators, and might be an indication of a corrupt way of distributing public resources. In 2003, the share of companies, which have participated in public tenders was more than 40% of the total, while some 5 years later it dropped to 10% (CSD 2009).

The energy sector and healthcare are the two biggest public procurers in the country with the most opaque practices. Approximately 40% of all procedures for the awarding of public procurement contracts in the energy sector for 2012 were non-competitive, encompassing the various negotiated procedures with or without the publication of a contract notice under the 2004 Act of Public Procurement (APP). If the contracts awarded without any public procurement procedure are added to this number, it becomes apparent that avoiding market competition is the rule rather than the exception in the energy sector (Stefanov et al. 2011).

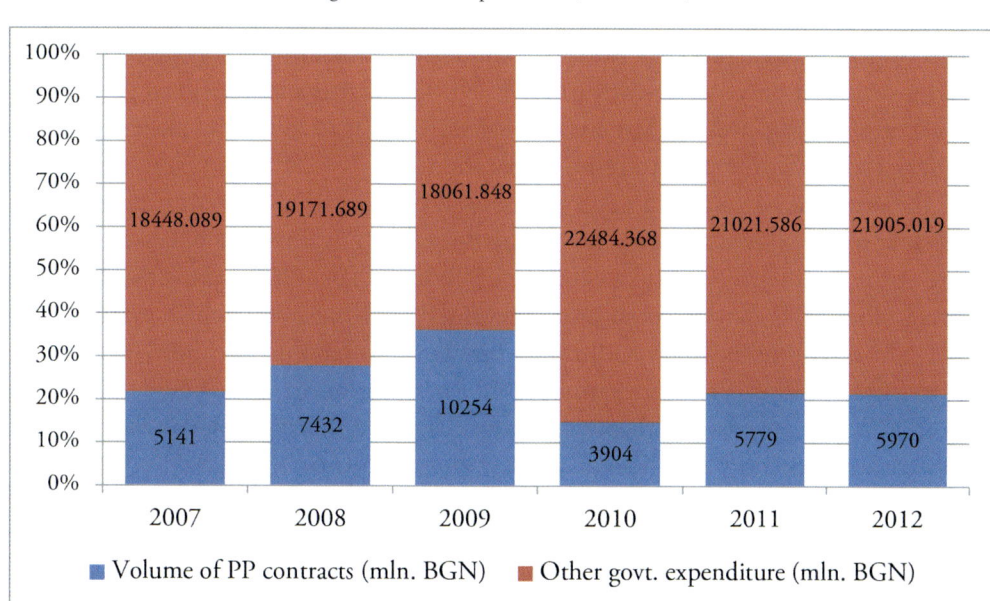

Figure 5. Volume of public procurement contracts as a share of all governmental expenditure (2007-2012).

Source: National Statistical Institute.

Despite the availability of many oversight institutions in public procurement the number of public procurement deals with violations of the law uncovered by the Public Financial Inspection Agency (PFIA) remain very high (**Table 2**). Although PFIA provides data on inspections and violations annually, there is no consistency between the meaning and the presentation of the data. As a result, both data collection and data comparison are difficult. The capacity of the Agency to tackle problematic public procurement increases, but its deterrence and prevention effects are very limited and violations continue to be wide spread. One reason is the constant political interference in the work of the agency in particular on bigger public procurement contracts. Hence the agency tends to focus on smaller public procurement deals, which have limited downside risks for the public exchequer.

Table 2. Concluded public procurement contracts per year (volume), (2007-2012).

Year	Total volume of the concluded PP contracts (million BGN)	Volume of the inspected PP contracts (million BGN)	Volume of the PP contracts with discovered violations (million BGN)
2012	5,970	2,044	1,488
2011	5,779	1,459	1,060
2010	3,904	2,203	1,191
2009	10,254	1,084	660
2008	7,432	636	306
2007	5,141	1,031	601

Source: PPA Annual Reports; PFIA Annual Reports 2013.

1.8. Separation private – public

The weak division between private and public could be traced back to the widespread perception that state property belongs to nobody (instead of belonging to everybody). Various cases of power abuse at various levels, in particular as relates to perks such as office cars, security, and housing have revealed that Bulgarian politicians have very little understanding for the private-public separation.

The attempts to create an appropriate legal basis for the separation of private and public interests started several years before Bulgaria's accession to the EU in 2007, as a part of the legal harmonization with the EU body of law. The result is the Conflict of Interest Prevention and Ascertainment Act (CIPAA) from 2009, which defines in legal terms the situations in which public office holders may have private interests preventing them from fulfilling their duties impartially. The application of the new rules has taken a long time, as citizens, politicians and administration do not have the understanding of disclosing potential conflicts of interest and addressing the issue. So far there has been one recorded case, in which an MP has disclosed a conflict of interest while voting for a proposed law. Officials often have a private business, so in order to ensure the formal separation from their private interests they transfer their business to relatives.

1.9. Relation formal/informal institutions

There is very high degree of informality in the Bulgarian economy and the public sector institutions. Each government since 1998 has been known for different informal circles of powerful friends, which have influenced its decisions without being part of the formal institutions. Key political leaders have shown clear disrespect for formal institutions, e.g. by not appearing in Parliament although being members.

The Bulgarian economy is characterised by a high degree of informality, which dates back to central planning when all private sector activity was prohibited. Tax evasion continues to be widespread. According to CSD's Hidden Economy Index, hidden economy has decreased steadily since 2002 but remains very high. Informal labour and tax relations are largely socially accepted in the country (CSD 2013b, p. 9). In 2012, 9 % of the employed in Bulgaria reported paying social security contributions at the minimal threshold legally required for their profession although the sum of their remuneration was higher. Another 13 % reported paying social security contributions on the sum stated in their contract, although the total sum of their remuneration was higher. According to different sources the size of the hidden economy is estimated at 10-35 % of GDP (Nonchev et al. 2011).

1.10. Accountability and rule of law

While transparency has increased steadily in Bulgaria in the past decade, accountability and the rule of law remain low. This is evidenced also by the continuous implementation of a specific mechanism by the EC to monitor the country's progress on rule of law and the reform of the judiciary. The structure of the Bulgarian judiciary does not allow public oversight and accountability. In cases of malpractice, the other branches of power cannot intervene and/or at least provide checks and balances. It has only been since Bulgaria's EU accession in 2007 that the EC pressed for the introduction of more reporting requirements for the judiciary. The EC has turned the spotlight on the Supreme Judicial Council as the body responsible for ensuring a more effective functioning of the judiciary. However, change is slow as also evidenced by the rising number of complaints and won trials against Bulgaria before the European Court of Justice. While resignations among high-level administrators, their prosecution and court trials against politicians and oligarchs have become more frequent in recent years, the sentences are rare, and their enforcement - even rarer. Public investigations have often been started more as a way to compromise a political opponent than as a tool for achieving justice.

2. Results beyond the empirical assessment: areas of policy change

The lessons learnt from the Bulgarian country case study confirm the findings that corruption is a multi-dimensional phenomenon, which is difficult to target through policy instruments. It demonstrates that there are many factors at play, which influence the governance regime and corrupt behaviour, and that changes are unlikely to occur in a revolutionary fashion.

The case study suggests that moving governance from its current state to the borderline might be more difficult and require a longer time-span and more intensive efforts. Areas of change that would both benefit anti-corruption and further societal change include the following policy areas:

2.1. E-government

Adoption of EU government and legislation standards has introduced new challenges to the administration and the operation of the government. Failure to adequately cope with this includes creating huge amounts of administrative turnover without the matching capacity of the administration to handle a different and increasing document turnover. For quite a long time it has been argued that implementation of e-government would in large part be highly beneficial for a multitude of reasons: simplification of administrative procedures in all areas, better and more efficient control, lower discretionary power for officials, higher transparency at all levels of government, etc. Efforts aimed at structuring this policy have been slowed down both by lack of administrative capacity and, more importantly, by the countering interest of the administration. This is why government since the mid-2000s have promised rapid results but have only been able to deliver great expenses and bad functioning elements of e-government subsystems.

2.2. Law enforcement reform

This is an element of governance that has been at the centre of public and political attention for years and yet an area of marginal progress. Key targets of reforms should be ensuring real effective independence of the judiciary, ensuring proper forms of accountability that would not limit but enforce independence and achieving higher levels of efficiency in the operation of the system. Currently the formal independence of the system seems to block reforms efforts; this is further reinforced by real forms of political dependence that fosters stability and lack of interest to change the status quo. According to many experts a more radical change is necessary and this would include changes in the Bulgarian Constitution.

2.3. Health and pension system reform

Both systems are currently heavily dependent on administrative and political decisions. The interests of clients (services) are not matched with contributions; as a result revenues are far behind expenses and only budget transfers keep the systems functioning and elementary subsistence level. This gives the political class leverage in times of elections and does not permit a sustainable development based on endogenous factors. Both systems (in view of people who do not contribute in full or on regular basis) tend to generate substantial amounts of 'grey' behaviour. In this respect, in addition to other aspects, reforms should aim at matching contributions and benefits and limit discretionary power of officials and the political class.

2.4. Anti-monopoly legislation

The interconnections between political power and the business sector have resulted in pieces of legislation which provide comparative advantages to specific business interests. Such cases have been especially difficult to deal with as these linkages generate resources for even greater state capture. In this respect the resource necessary (and in shortage) is political will.

References

Angarev, P. (2009) 'Ахмед Доган: Властта е в моитеръце!' (Ahmed Dogan: The power is in my hands!) *Capital Newspaper*, 26 Jun 2009. Available from: <http://www.capital.bg/vestnikut/kapital_prim/2009/06/25/743444_ahmed_dogan_vlastta_e_v_moite_ruce/>

Center for Prevention and Countering Corruption and Organized Crime (CPCCOC) (2013) First Report on the Project 'Decision Model in the Sphere of Public Procurements'. Available from: <http://borkor.government.bg/bg/page/437#>

Center for the Study of Democracy (CSD) (2007) 'Monitoring Anti-corruption Reforms in Bulgaria'. Available from: <http://www.csd.bg/artShow.php?id=8406>

Center for the Study of Democracy (CSD) (2009) 'Crime without Punishment: Countering Corruption and Organized Crime in Bulgaria'. Available from: <http://www.csd.bg/artShow.php?id=9583>

Center for the Study of Democracy (CSD) (2012) 'Serious and Organised Crime Threat Assessment 2010 – 2011'. Available from: <http://www.csd.bg/artShow.php?id=15991>

Center for the Study of Democracy (CSD) (2013a) 'Policy Brief 43: Corruption and Anti-corruption in Bulgaria (2012-2013)'. Available from: <http://www.csd.bg/artShow.php?id=16731>

Center for the Study of Democracy (CSD) (2013b) 'Policy Brief 37: The Hidden Economy in Bulgaria 2011-2012'. Available from: <http://www.csd.bg/artShow.php?id=16342>

della Porta, D., Pizzorno, A. and Donaldson, J. (1996) 'The Business Politicians: Reflections from a Study of Political Corruption,' *The Corruption of Politics and the Politics of Corruption Journal of Law and Society* Vol. 23, No. 1, pp. 73-94. Available from: <http://www.jstor.org/stable/1410468>

European Commission (2012) 'Report from the Commission to the European Parliament and the Council on Progress in Bulgaria under the Cooperation and Verification Mechanism'. Available from: <http://ec.europa.eu/cvm/docs/com_2012_411_en.pdf>

European Commission (2014) 'Report from the Commission to the European Parliament and the Council on Progress in Bulgaria under the Cooperation and Verification Mechanism'. Available from: <http://ec.europa.eu/cvm/docs/com_2014_36_en.pdf>

Global Integrity (2010) 'The Global Integrity Report: Integrity Scorecard on Bulgaria'. Available from: <https://www.globalintegrity.org/global/the-global-integrity-report-2010/bulgaria/>

Gounev, Ph. and Bezlov, T. (2012) 'Examining the Links between Organised Crime and Corruption'. *European Commission, DG Home*. Available from: <http://www.csd.bg/fileSrc.php?id=20428>

International Budget Partnership (IBP) (2013) Open Budget Survey 2012. Available from: <http://internationalbudget.org/wp-content/uploads/OBI2012-Report-English.pdf>

Kaufmann, D., Kraay, A. and Mastruzzi, M. (2013) Worldwide Governance Indicators. Available from: <http://info.worldbank.org/governance/wgi/index.aspx#home>

Mungiu-Pippidi, A. et al. (2011) Contextual Choices in Fighting Corruption: Lessons Learned, NORAD, Report 4/2011. Available from: <http://www.norad.no/en/tools-and-publications/publications/publication?key=383808>

Mungiu-Pippidi, A. (2013) The Good, the bad and the ugly: controlling corruption in the European Union, *ANTICORRP*. Available from: <http://www.againstcorruption.eu/wp-content/uploads/2013/03/ANTICORRP-Policy-Paper-on-Lessons-Learnt-1_protected1.pdf>

Nikolaeva, V, (2013) Торнадо в екологията (Tornado in the Ecology) *Capital Newspaper*. 1 Aug 2013. Available from: <http://www.capital.bg/politika_i_ikonomika/bulgaria/2013/08/01/2114873_tornado_v_ekologiiata/>

Nonchev, A. et al. (2011) The Hidden Economy in Bulgaria and the Global Economic Crisis, *Center for the Study of Democracy*. Available from: <http://www.csd.bg/artShow.php?id=15798>

Pashev, K. (2007) Corruption in the Healthcare Sector in Bulgaria, *Center for the Study of Democracy*. Available from: <http://www.csd.bg/artShow.php?id=8843>

Public Procurement Agency (PPA) (2012) Annual Report 2012. Available from: <http://www.aop.bg/fckedit2/user/File/bg/agency/Annual_report_2012-final-1.pdf>

Stefanov, R. et al. (2011) Energy and Good Governance in Bulgaria: Trends and Policy Options, *Center for the Study of Democracy*. Available from: <http://www.csd.bg/artShow.php?id=15499>

3. The Unlikely Achiever: Rwanda

ALESSANDRO BOZZINI

Rwanda has recently been praised by a lot of donors and development experts for its recovery from the 1994 genocide, sustained economic growth and improvement of many socioeconomic indicators, partly achieved thanks to massive aid flows. A key feature of Rwanda's progress is often considered to be governance and particularly anti-corruption: the country is generally regarded as one of the least corrupt in Africa and a success story in reducing corruption. This paper aims to analyse the state of corruption and the wider governance context in Rwanda, attempting to evaluate whether the country's governance regime is an open access order characterized by ethical universalism, a limited access order dominated by particularism, or a hybrid. After providing an overview of the country's anti-corruption framework, the paper analyses a number of governance aspects and assesses the incidence of different forms of petty and grand corruption in a bid to ascertain the extent to which claims of Rwanda as an anti-corruption success story are well-founded.[1]

Rwanda made international headlines in 1994 when the genocide, one of the worst tragedies since the end of World War II, claimed an appalling number of victims, left the country shattered and exposed the international community's indifference. In spite of the sombre image associated with such a calamity, Rwanda has been able to change its reputation in recent years and, thanks to sustained high growth rates, has increasingly been seen as a development model. Improved governance and political stability are often quoted as key reasons for the country's economic success.

This paper builds on the author's first-hand experience living and working as an anti-corruption practitioner in Rwanda, on direct observation, on countless informal interactions and exchanges of views, as well as on a number of targeted, formal interviews of a diverse range of local and foreign resource persons and a review of primary and secondary literature.

1. State of governance

Rwanda is a small landlocked country located in central-Eastern Africa. A former Belgian colony, its population, according to the 2012 census, is estimated at around

---

[1] This chapter builds on, and further develops, Bozzini, A. (2013). Successes and limitations of a top-down approach to governance: the case of anti-corruption in Rwanda. ISPI-Istituto per gli Studi di Politica Internazionale, Milan, Italy.
[2] The list of interviews conducted by the author for this chapter can be found in the full version of the report at: http://anticorrp.eu/publications/background-paper-on-rwanda/.

11 million spread over 26,338 km², making it Africa's most densely populated country. Its GDP is estimated at $15.74 billion while its GDP per capita is estimated at $ 1,500 (CIA World Factbook 2012). Despite progress, 44.9% of the population still lives in poverty and 24% in extreme poverty (National Institute of Statistics 2012), while the UNDP Human Development Index 2012 ranks Rwanda 167th out of 187 countries.

Since the 1994 Genocide, Rwanda has made remarkable progress in many areas. Even though many indicators of progress are based on surveys carried out within the country, which raises doubts on the reliability of the findings given the perceived 'high degree of self-censorship among the Rwandan peasant population,' (Ingelaere 2010, p. 53) the country is at peace and is often considered 'among the most stable on the continent'. Its GDP has registered an average annual growth rate of 7-8% since 2003, hitting 8% in 2012, making it the world's 10th fastest-growing economy in the 2000-10 decade. Extreme poverty is reported to have decreased dramatically. The World Bank Doing Business reports indicate that Rwanda improved its world ranking by almost 100 positions from 150th in 2008 to 52 in 2013. A number of socio-economic indicators, including school enrolment, life expectancy, child mortality and prevalence of HIV, have significantly improved (World Bank's 2009-12 World Development Indicators) and the Human Development Index has reflected such improvements.

An important contribution to these achievements has been made by foreign aid, which has been injected in large quantities by donors since the aftermath of the genocide, making Rwanda a so-called 'aid darling'; due to the Government's ability to use 'donor-friendly language and positioning' and donors' 'desire for African success stories' (Zorbas 2011).

2. The key to Rwanda's perceived success

One of the key reasons behind Rwanda's improvements of the last few years, as well as one of the elements which explain donors' willingness to provide high aid volumes, is considered to be governance. This is usually understood in a way that focuses more on the authority and decision-making, rather than accountability: the Government of Rwanda is commended for its high degree of organization, its capacity to manage resources efficiently and its focus on delivering results. Within Rwanda's governance agenda, perhaps the most celebrated feature is the control of corruption and the country is largely praised for its commitment to fight against graft and for the success that such a fight has reaped: indeed, the majority of analysts, international organizations and business people now consider Rwanda as one of the least corrupt countries in Africa as well as a success story in the fight against corruption.

Most observers would say that a key reason behind Rwanda's progress is the Government's 'political will' to fight corruption, a commitment from the country's top leadership to pursue this fight as one of the national priorities. This has resulted in a number of new laws and institutions. The key legal document is law n° 23/2003 on prevention and repression of corruption and related offences but a number of other laws include commitments to the fight against corruption, particularly the penal code in articles 220-27, while Rwanda has also signed and ratified most international anti-corruption conventions. Institutionally, the Government established several bodies including the Office of the Ombudsman, the Rwanda Public Procurement Authority, the Office of the Auditor General, the Anti-Corruption Unit in the Rwanda Revenue Authority and the Public Procurement Appeals Commission. Moreover, a number of high national authorities must disclose their assets, in 2011 the Public Accounts Committee was established within the Parliament and in July 2012 the Government approved the National Policy to fight against corruption, which formalizes the so-called 'zero tolerance' approach. More recently, a Whistleblower Protection Law was approved in September 2012, while many public institutions have codes of conduct. Furthermore, both politicians and civil servants have been prosecuted when allegations of corruption were brought against them, though some cite these cases as being used for excising political opponents.

Rwanda's progress is perhaps best illustrated by the country's performance in the World Bank control of corruption index which shows a clear improvement from 2006 to 2011, as shown below.

Figure 1. Evolution of Rwanda's 'Control of Corruption' score from 2006 to 2011.

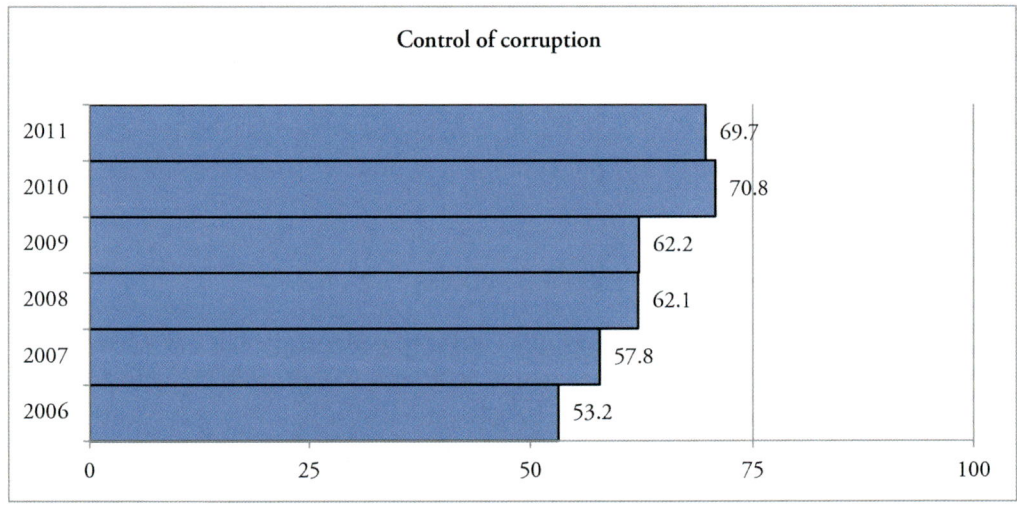

Source: World Bank Worldwide Governance Indicators, Control of Corruption.

Local officials, foreign observers and international organizations almost always mention this successful control of corruption in their interviews and reports with little questioning of whether the official narrative might or might not be exaggerated. In nearly all situations, however, corruption refers to bribes, and patrimonialism by rulers is hardly discussed.

2.1. Power distribution

Power in Rwanda is unevenly distributed; however, it is difficult to identify which group or network is the most powerful. Some would indicate that Tutsis generally have more power than Hutus (Cooke 2011, p. 12). This is an extremely sensitive issue, given the past of ethnic tensions and hatred which culminated in the 1994 genocide and is a difficult topic to investigate because the current authorities are extremely strict in preventing any discourse or research based on ethnic groups. Others would say that the most powerful group is the Rwandan Patriotic Front (RPF), the ruling party. Some would say English-speaking Rwandans (mostly former Tutsi refugees in Anglophone countries such as Uganda and Kenya who returned to the country after the genocide) are advantaged in public administration and private business over French-speaking citizens. Finally, some observers interviewed indicated President Paul Kagame himself as the dominating figure, deducing that his personal allies and aides would be the most powerful group in the country.

Each of these views can be at least partly refuted. Those disagreeing with the ethnic interpretation would point to the fact that there are Hutus in prominent positions in the government, albeit in largely ceremonial positions, in the military and in business. Those rejecting the view of a dominant party would note that some Ministers are affiliated to parties other than the RPF, as the Constitution requires that the largest party holds no more than 50% of cabinet posts. Those in disagreement with the language explanation would simply say that the de facto decision to promote English instead of French is strategically motivated in the context of Rwanda's membership of the East African Community. Finally, one could easily say that the President is powerful just because he is popular.

All these counterarguments are partly true. However, the RPF does enjoy a dominant position. While the current Government is formally a coalition and several parties are officially registered and functioning, there is little doubt that Rwanda is de facto a one-party State and the dominant position of the RPF is quite evident.

Several interviewees indicated that those top politicians who are not from the RPF often have a party member as deputy to monitor their actions; party membership is often considered helpful to be recruited in public administration; the limited resources, virtually no visibility and almost no presence in remote areas of the other parties; RPF's strong, and in some sectors dominant, position in the economy; limited space for other groups to express dissent including from abroad ; RPF's widespread presence in the field down to the most local level, through structures that 'mimic those of the state [...] with the result that the lines between ruling party and state are blurred' (see Purdeková 2011); and the extremely large membership of the party. This situation does not change with elections, as in recent years the RPF has largely won them all: Kagame, as RPF leader, won presidential elections in 2003 and 2010 both with massive scores (see IFES 2014). Interviewees expect this to continue, as the debate around the presidential elections in 2017 is essentially a debate about who the RPF candidate will be, as whoever he/she will be, will be the President. As several respondents put it, 'the party and the Government are the same thing' in Rwanda.

2.2. Accountability bodies and mechanisms

In the case of the five sources used for Transparency International's CPI score for Rwanda, the highest score is the World Economic Forum executive opinion survey, which mostly looks at the likeliness of firms to make undocumented extra payments or bribes. However, the sources which look more at transparency and accountability, give Rwanda significantly lower scores. The 2012 edition of the Mo Ibrahim Index, probably Africa's most important assessment on governance, ranks Rwanda at the middle of its ranking, 23rd out of 52 countries, with a score of 53.5 (on a scale where 0 is the worst and 100 is the best). All these assessments point to a potential contradiction: a country which has achieved good results in controlling corruption but whose accountability bodies and mechanisms are extremely weak. Indeed the media, civil society, the parliament and the judiciary play a limited accountability role in Rwanda.

2.3. Parliament

The parliament is dominated by the ruling party, the RPF, which won the parliamentary elections in 2008 and 2013 by a large margin (see IFES 2014). Other parties are more allies than opponents and all parties (except those which were not allowed to register; see Longman 2011) are constitutionally mandated to be members of a consultative forum which provides a framework to discuss and then agree on political proposals. The Government claims that Rwanda's 'consensual democracy' is a successful model to unify the country, avoid conflicts and agree on policies, but the absence of a formal opposition weakens the Parliament's potential as an accountability institution. The Parliament has strengthened its accountability role in the last few years: the recently created Public Accounts Committee is working hard to summon politicians requesting them to explain alleged irregularities related to public funds. As an interviewee pointed out, parliamentarians are accountable to the RPF and to the President; because they know they 'owe' their position to the party and its leader.

2.4. Media

The Genocide era Government tragically used the infamous Radio Télévision Libre des Mille Collines (RTLM) as a tool to spread ethnic hatred and incite violence and the current Government is still reluctant to grant press freedom and accept open dissent in the media. This is consistently certified by a wide range of observers such as Reporters Without Borders, whose 2013 world press freedom index scores Rwanda 161st out of 179 (and declining) (see Reporters Without Borders 2013). The Mo Ibrahim Index confirms this assessment, ranking it 48th out of 52 African countries. Also, some journalists have been murdered in unclear circumstances and many engage in self-censorship (see Freedom House 2011). Radio is the most popular media and new stations have started broadcasting in recent years, but while there are shows in which people call in to report their problems, radios usually avoid controversial issues, let alone government criticism, and are closely watched. As a result, the Rwandan media do not play a strong role in scrutiny and accountability and individual cases of corruption often make headlines, but politically sensitive issues, or cases involving the top leadership of the country, are completely missing, while investigative journalism is discouraged and is virtually non-existent.

2.5. Civil society

The situation in Rwanda with civil society is similar to that of the media. The Government, despite granting formal registration to most national and foreign NGOs, is reluctant to consider civil society organizations (CSOs) as full political actors, seeing them as mere service providers, and allows limited space for them to question and challenge public policies and programs. CSOs are generally weak, highly dependent on foreign donors and have little capacity. They also often have limited independence from the political power, to the extent that they 'are almost unanimously tied into or legitimized by Government in some fashion' (see Gready 2011) and even though some 'independent CSOs and NGOs exist at national level [...] they react to the Government's distrust with self-censorship and therefore make little impact' (the Bertelsmann Transformation Index from 2012 give Rwanda's 'civil society participation' a 3 out of 10). Most local NGOs see themselves as partners of the Government rather than counterweight or watchdogs.

2.6. Judiciary and the Ombudsman

Rwanda's accountability institutions also include an ombudsman: an office whose presence is positive in itself and which is playing a visible role in sensitizing the population about the negative consequences of corruption. However, the fact that for many years the Chief Ombudsman's position was held by a 'top ideologue' and founder of the ruling party raises doubt about the independence of the institution, in spite of his reputation as a person of high moral standards and integrity. Similar concerns of limited independence apply to the Office of the Auditor General and to the judiciary: they tend to track relatively minor issues and hardly ever tackle cases of grand corruption involving high-level members of the ruling party, the Government or the army (see Cooke 2011, p. 13) and when they do so there are often rumours that the main rationale is to punish those who fell out of line (see Bertelsmann Foundation 2012, p. 26).

2.7. Independence of state bureaucracy

Rwanda's oft-praised ability to manage projects, programs and donor funds would not be possible without a skilled bureaucracy made up of officials recruited based on merit. At the same time, there are also claims that influential positions are held by RPF members or loyalists.

Both assertions are correct. The Government has introduced many measures to improve transparency in recruitment and to ensure that the best candidates get jobs based on merit. These include guidelines on timing and modalities for publishing a vacancy and holding job interviews but also include the provision that a candidate who feels he/she has been treated unfairly can report the case to the Ombudsman or the Public Service Commission, the latter being an institution created precisely in a bid to guarantee neutral recruitment and performance-based evaluation. Despite limited technical capacity in some fields, Rwandan public administration is relatively efficient, recruitment practices have improved over time and most technical positions, as well as most low- to middle-ranking officials, seem to be indeed recruited based on candidate merit. However, top officials tend to be politically appointed and some interviewees also mentioned cases of politically-influenced recruitment.

2.8. Separation of public and private

Some private companies are closely linked to and intertwined with the RPF and thus with the Government and the state. Today there are three holdings, or conglomerates, of 'party-statals'. The largest one, Crystal Ventures Limited (CVL), formerly known as Tri-Star Investments, is a private holding company fully owned by RPF. Having grown out of the production unit of the then-rebel army RPA during the 1990-94 war, which eventually put an end to the Genocide; Tri-Star got the bulk of its initial funding from wealthy supporters from the Rwandan diaspora. Today, CVL holds a majority stake in 11 companies and a minority stake in several joint ventures, ranging from civil works to real estate, telecommunications and security services, most of which are the leading national company in their sectors. The group's 2009 turnover represented over 3% of Rwanda's GDP.

The second conglomerate, Horizon Group Limited, is often referred to in Kigali as 'the army's company': having received initial capital from the Military Medical Insurance (MMI) and the Military Micro Finance Cooperative Society (ZIGAMA-CSS), it is now a private firm but is considered the army's investment arm and its CEO is seconded by the army. The third consortium is Rwanda Investment Group (RIG), a holding company created in 2006 at the instigation of the Government, which is now a holding with both public and private shareholders whose purpose is to raise funds to invest primarily in the construction and energy sectors.

While most people in Kigali know that some companies are controlled by RPF and the army, and while party officials say 'it is no secret' that they run a number of companies and big investments (Kagire 2012), still the websites of the three holdings do not mention RPF anywhere, so this is a transparency issue. The second issue is the potential favouritism that these companies might benefit from. There is a general perception among many local and foreign entrepreneurs that CVL and Horizon companies enjoy preferential treatment when they compete for public contracts, to the extent that some entrepreneurs said that when they see that one of those companies bid, they 'do not bother bidding'. RPF officials and observers who support the party's role in the private sector deny any favouritism and point to the several bids that their companies have lost as well as to the competition they face from local and foreign companies. It is true that Crystal Ventures and other RPF-controlled companies do not win all the contracts they bid for, that the RPF is very careful to avoid a 'winner takes all' image and that Rwanda has made progress in procurement practices and has a comprehensive legal framework in this field. At the same time, in a country where accountability bodies are weak and not fully independent, it is hard to believe that members of a public tendering agency, for example a District, who usually have strong links with the ruling party, are not tempted to favour companies linked to the same ruling party.

Another area of potential favouritism is taxation: a researcher who was able to examine the list of top taxpayers in 2010 (no longer available on Rwanda Revenue Authority's website) reports that 'only 11 party-statals (less than half of the 25) were among the top 307 large taxpayers in 2010' and that the CVL subsidiary in the food processing sector, Inyange, whose market share is over 85%, 'is not among the top taxpayers' while 'its two immediate competitors [...], which have smaller market concentrations, do appear on this list' (Gökgür 2012, p. 27).

While the presence of such party-statals is the main issue and concern: there is a general perception that proximity to the ruling party is a key element for an entrepreneur to have economic success: it might not be indispensable, as there are some businesses with no link to the party and the Government's commitment to the country's economic development is genuine, but many businesspeople reportedly decide to affiliate with the RPF or to show their support as they feel this could somehow benefit their business. Whether or to which extent this is true is obviously very difficult to assess, but this widespread perception confirms the blurring between public and private. Fortunately, it is uncommon for politicians and officials to use public funds to cover their private expenses.

To conclude on this complex and controversial issue, it is safe to say that in Rwanda the state, the Government, the ruling party and the private sector are not entirely separate entities, with obvious problems in terms of separation of powers, risks of favouritism and limited transparency; such a blurring between private and public is a key feature of patrimonialism.

2.9. Service delivery

Corruption in service delivery is the subject of tight scrutiny by the Government, of harsh sanctions and of calls for integrity as well as sensitization campaigns. Indeed, the widely cited 'political will' of the Rwandan Government to fight against corruption is mostly visible in this field. Overall, services such as health, education, water or issue of documents are provided evenly and impartially, with corruption being the exception and not the rule; fear of sanctions or of retaliation by authorities may lead to under-reporting of corruption cases, but it is safe to say that corruption in this field is not institutionalized and that the overall goal is to cater to everybody.

Despite the overall positive situation, petty corruption is however far from eradicated and studies show that the police and local authorities tend to be the institutions most exposed to such practices, though they have all showed progress in the last few years and are comparatively much less affected than their counterparts in the East African region.

Similarly, embezzlement of public funds seems to be quite uncommon and taxpayers' money as well as foreign aid are generally well managed and usually reach the beneficiaries as intended. The efficiency and integrity with which authorities tend to manage public funds is mentioned by most donors in Kigali as the main reason why they provide generous levels of aid to Rwanda.

2.10. Transparency

On top of the limited role played by the accountability organs and bodies, the concept of transparency, which is one of the key tools in the fight against corruption, is yet to fully develop in Rwanda. Indeed, in spite of efforts to disclose more information about the authorities and their activities and despite a recently adopted Access to Information law, the transparency of key issues remains limited: the Open Budget Survey 2012, developed by the International Budget Partnership in cooperation with a local NGO, gives Rwanda a score of 8 (down from 11 in 2010, on a scale from 1 to 100 where 100 is the best score), which is much lower than the global average of 43 for all the 100 countries surveyed and is also significantly worse than the other countries in the region. Interestingly, the country which is usually ranked, by far, as East Africa's least corrupt, appears in this survey as the region's least transparent.

Politicians have to disclose their assets to the Ombudsman, but many believe that some top leaders do not include some of their assets in such declarations knowing that they will not be investigated. Procurement and mineral trade from bordering conflict-ridden Eastern Congo are also areas where transparency is somehow limited. Transparency in elections has also been questioned and there are allegations that the Government might have altered the proportions of votes received by some parties (Greene 2011, p. 17; Longman 2011, p. 39-40).

2.11. Citizen participation

Citizen participation is often considered another key element to prevent and reduce corruption. Again, Rwanda is a paradox, as the relatively low level of corruption is matched by an even lower level of citizen participation. Indeed ordinary citizens are reluctant to engage in the public sphere and the Government itself has acknowledged this challenge, thus stating in official documents the objective of encouraging more participation. At the same time, citizen participation is often 'directed and controlled' by the authorities (Bertelsmann Foundation 2012, pp. 22-3). It is still noticeable that the only public demonstrations in the last few years have been pro-governmental, raising doubts that they were actually organized by the Government itself.

Interestingly, some observe that limited participation is nothing new in Rwanda; this would be due to the fact that, as a consequence of civil war, exile and the Genocide, other forms of constituency and shelter have weakened (traditional and family ties, regional and religious identities) and 'historically therefore Rwandans have tended to revere political power and are passive in political matters' (Kayumba 2013).

Conclusions

Incidence of corruption in Rwanda is undoubtedly lower than in its regional neighbours, but perhaps the country is not as successful as some believe. The Government's oft-mentioned 'political will to fight against corruption', seems to be mostly a will to fight monetary forms at low to middle levels. Consequently, there have been achievements in controlling bribery, mismanagement and embezzlement, particularly at lower levels. The key corruption problem that remains in Rwanda is favouritism; authorities are keen and determined to curb administrative corruption but are much less eager to tackle political corruption.

Secondly, the fight against corruption (at least the monetary kind) has followed a top-down approach: the establishment of new laws and institutions, the sensitization campaigns and public calls for integrity have mostly come from the highest levels of Government, including from the President himself. While this is positive and important, it has severe limitations. In particular, it intrinsically excludes those forms that the top leadership does not want to fight such as influence peddling and political favouritism. Moreover, this approach is unlikely to be sustainable in the long term, as it stems from a number of individual leaders rather than being rooted in strong institutions, transparency mechanisms and citizen participation. Indeed, the fact that more and more citizens abstain from corruption seems to be mostly due to fear of harsh punishment rather than to cultural or behavioural change.

Thirdly, the governance system in Rwanda is somewhere between ethical universalism and particularism, and a borderline case between open access and limited access order. While formal laws and policies are clearly striving towards universalism, and are often comprehensive and commendable, there remains a certain level of informality. Similarly, the weakness of accountability bodies, limited citizen participation, unequal power distribution and blurring of public and private mean that Rwanda is far from a fully open access order. It is therefore extremely difficult to give an ultimate answer to the question of 'whether corruption is the exception or whether it is the norm' (Mungiu-Pippidi 2006, p. 91). Monetary forms of corruption and especially bribery exist but are the exception to the norm, other forms such as favouritism and abuse of power by the Government and the ruling party are more common and are ultimately to a great extent socially accepted as a rule of the game.

A number of lessons can be learnt from the analysis of the state of governance and corruption in Rwanda. First, corruption should be defined in broad terms as encompassing all its forms, including non-monetary ones, as a country might have low incidence of some forms and high incidence of others. Moreover, the case of Rwanda suggests that petty or administrative corruption can in some cases be a very different issue from grand or political corruption, as curbing the former does not necessarily mean reducing the latter. In addition, and perhaps most importantly, Rwanda shows that relative success in fighting bribery is not necessarily associated, as many would assume, with high levels of accountability, transparency and citizen participation. This confirms the need, when investigating corruption, to analyse the broader governance context of a country.

References

Bertelsmann Foundation (2012) 'Rwanda Country Report', *Bertelsmann Transformation Index 2012*. Available from: <www.bti-project.org/country-reports/esa/rwa>

CIA (Central Intelligence Agency) (2012) *World Factbook: Rwanda*. Available from <https://www.cia.gov/library/publications/the-world-factbook/geos/rw.html>

Cooke, J. G. (2011) 'Rwanda - Assessing risks to stability', *Center for Strategic and International Studies*, Washington, DC. Available from: <http://csis.org/files/publication/110623_Cooke_Rwanda_Web.pdf>

Freedom House (2011) *Freedom on the Net 2011 – Rwanda*. Available from: <www.freedomhouse.org/sites/default/files/inline_images/Rwanda_FOTN2011.pdf>

Gökgür, N. (2012) 'Rwanda's ruling party-owned enterprises: Do they enhance or impede development?' *Institute of Development Policy and Management*. Available from: <http://ideas.repec.org/p/iob/dpaper/2012003.html>

Gready, P. (2011) 'Beyond 'You're with us or against us': Civil Society and Policymaking in Post-Genocide Rwanda'. In S. Straus and L. Waldorf (eds.) *Remaking Rwanda - State Building and Human Rights after Mass Violence*. Madison: The University of Wisconsin Press, pp. 87-102

Green, E. (2011) 'Patronage as Institutional Choice: Evidence from Rwanda and Uganda', *Comparative Politics*, 43(4), pp. 421-38

IFES (International Foundation for Electora Systems (2014) *Election Guide: Rwanda*. Available from <http://www.electionguide.org/countries/id/180/>

Ingelaere, B. (2010) 'Do we understand life after genocide?' *African Studies Review*, 53(1), pp. 41-59

International Budget Partnership (2012). *Open Budget Survey 2012*. Available from: <http://internationalbudget.org/wp-content/uploads/OBI2012-Report-English.pdf>

Kagire, E. (2012) 'Our businesses are clean, says RPF', *The East African*, 12 Oct. 2012. Available from <http://www.theeastafrican.co.ke/Rwanda/News/Our-businesses-are-clean-says-RPF/-/1433218/1532008/-/7j64skz/-/index.html>

Kayumba, C. (2013) 'In Rwanda, you toe the official line, or live and die a pauper or in exile', *The East African*, 12 July. Available from: <http://www.theeastafrican.co.ke/Rwanda/Opinion/In-Rwanda-toe-official-line-or-live-die-a-pauper-or-in-exile----/-/1433246/1912628/-/4bo83b/-/index.html>

Longman, T. (2011) 'Limitations to Political Reform: The Undemocratic Nature of Transition in Rwanda'. In S. Straus and L. Waldorf (eds.) *Remaking Rwanda - State Building and Human Rights after Mass Violence*. Madison: The University of Wisconsin Press, pp. 25-47

Mo Ibrahim Foundation (2012) *Ibrahim Index of African Governance 2012*. Available from: <www.moibrahimfoundation.org/iiag>

Mungiu-Pippidi, A. (2006) 'Corruption: Diagnosis and Treatment', *Journal of Democracy*, 17(3), pp. 86-99

National Institute of Statistics (2012) *Third Integrated Household Living Conditions Survey (EICV3, Enquête Intégrale sur les Conditions de Vie des Ménages)*. Available from: <www.statistics.gov.rw>

Purdeková, A. (2011) "Even if I am not here, there are so many eyes': surveillance and state reach in Rwanda', *Journal of Modern African Studies*, 49(3), pp. 475-97

Reporters Without Borders (2013) *World press freedom index 2012*. Available from: <http://fr.rsf.org/IMG/pdf/classement_2013_gb-bd.pdf>

Transparency International (2012) *East Africa Bribery Index*. Available from: <www.tirwanda.org/images/stories/finalper cent20eabiper cent202012.pdf>

UNDP (2012) *Human Development Reports*. Available from: <http://hdr.undp.org/en/reports>

World Bank (2012) World Development Indicators 2009-12. Available from: <http://data.worldbank.org/counry/rwanda>

World Bank (2013) *Doing Business Reports*. Available from: <www.doingbusiness.org>

Zorbas, E. (2011) 'Aid Dependence and Policy Independence: Explaining the Rwandan Paradox'. In S. Straus and L. Waldorf (eds.) *Remaking Rwanda - State Building and Human Rights after Mass Violence*. Madison: The University of Wisconsin Press, pp. 103-17

4. Doubts and Lessons Learned from Qatar's Progress Towards Good Governance

LINA KHATIB[1]

Qatar is judged by international anti-corruption indices to be among the highest performing countries in the Middle East and North Africa (MENA). The Qatari government has streamlined its regulations regarding business practices and engaged in reforms from above that have liberalized the Qatari economy and increased its strength and viability. There are lessons to learn for other countries in such reforms. However, Qatar remains a neo-patrimonial absolute monarchy in which the state is not immune from private interests, and where the ruling family can bypass the rule of law. This chapter analyses the structures and mechanisms of Qatar's governance regime that reveal the contradictions inherent within the categories covered by corruption indices. In doing so, it suggests a number of shortcomings in the methodologies and scope of those indices as they specifically apply to Qatar, and poses a number of questions regarding the kind of information that is difficult to find but which is crucial to address in order to form a clearer picture of corruption and anti-corruption practices in Qatar. The author concludes that the absence of this information in the first place casts a shadow of doubt over the performance of Qatar in anti-corruption indices.

The richest country in the world in terms of GDP per capita, Qatar has been performing well in global anti-corruption indices. Qatar's score rose from 77.07 in the 2002 World Governance Indicators (WGI) Control of Corruption indicator to 83.73 in WGI 2012. Transparency International's Corruption Perceptions Index (CPI) 2012—which uses the same sources as WGI—also ranks Qatar as 27th in the world in terms of perceptions of anti-corruption, with a score of 68 (out of 100), making it the best performing country in the MENA region (See Transparency International 2012 CPI). However, before Qatar can be considered a case of good anti-corruption practice, one should consider how the indices define corruption. Current corruption indices do not cover the full spectrum of social allocation when measuring corruption, nor do they address the nature of the governance regime and its relationship with corruption in the countries assessed. For the purposes of this paper, corruption is defined as particular (non-universal) allocation of public goods due to abuse of influence, and control of corruption is defined as the capacity of a society to constrain abuse of

---

[1] The author thanks Jan Raudszus, Nuria Moya Guzman, and Lisa Buckmaster for their assistance with researching this chapter, and Larry Diamond and Stanford University for their support.

influence resulting in a social allocation diverging from ethical universalism (everyone treated similarly) (Mungiu-Pippidi 2006). Applying those definitions to the case of Qatar challenges its anti-corruption index rankings.

1. State of governance in Qatar

Qatar is a neo-patrimonial absolute monarchy with extreme particularism (O'Donnell 1996) in which the Emir reigns, rules, and has historically owned state institutions. The Emir has the authority to select ministers, dictate foreign and domestic policies, and control the economy (Yom and Gause 2012). The Al Thani family has ruled the country for decades, with the current Sheikh Tamim taking over from his father Sheikh Hamad in 2013, following Hamad's bloodless coup against his own father Sheikh Khalifa in 1995. Khalifa himself had deposed his uncle in a coup in 1972. Coups have been common in the history of Qatar, and make it less likely for rulers to share power equitably, due to the lack of trust even in own family members that accompanies such acts of power takeover. They also foster a culture of rentierism and distribution of resources to buy loyalty. The Al Thani family has institutionalized tribal and filial relationships through allocating government roles and resources to local tribal leaders and princes in return for their political backing. The family has also drawn the boundaries of the districts of modern Qatar according to tribal districts (Fromherz 2012).

Sheikh Hamad's rule was characterized by economic liberalization and an expanded foreign policy agenda, changing the public image of Qatar from a small state in the shadow of Saudi Arabia to one of the major players in the international relations and economics of the Middle East. This expansion has been supported by Qatar's wealth, with the country possessing the world's third largest gas field (Khatib 2013).

Qatar's wealth has enabled the ruling family to curb potential dissent. Domestically, wealth is distributed both to citizens at large as well to tribes, in the form of cash handouts and social and health service, and through the allocation of bureaucratic posts. Qataris enjoy free health services and education, a stipend of around $7000 per month per citizen, and almost guaranteed employment in the public sector (the unemployment rate is 1%). Tribal leaders are appointed in well-paid public posts (Rathmell and Schulze 2000). Wealth distribution has aided Qatar in avoiding the rise of popular discontent seen elsewhere in the Arab world.

However, the privileges given to Qatari citizens do not extend to the majority of the resident population in Qatar. The country is home to only around 250,000 Qatari nationals, with 80% of the total population being composed of expats from a wide variety of countries. Those expats possess restricted personal and economic rights. For example, all expats can only work under a 'kafala' (sponsorship) system that links their legal presence in Qatar to sponsored employment by a Qatari national. In the case of migrant workers performing low-income jobs, this system has allowed employers to deny workers basic rights like regular days off, access to health care, and equitable working environments. In this sense, the public allocation of resources only narrowly applies to Qatari citizens. Migrant workers have been effectively prevented from demanding further rights because of their dependency on Qatari sponsorship.

Qatari nationals, meanwhile, have developed a sense of dependency on the state, especially regarding employment. Although just over half of Qatari citizens (55%) who took part in the Qatar World Values Survey 2010 said that individuals should provide for mostly (24%) or exclusively (31%) of their economic needs, as opposed to the government, practice reveals a different pattern. Government services constitute 14% of Qatar's economic output, and the public sector is saturated (Berrebi et al. 2009) with public servants who cannot be fired, however inefficient they may be.

Dependency can be linked to a cultivated sense of entitlement that can easily be confused with satisfaction. A Qatari national who regards public employment as a 'right' and who is almost guaranteed to have this 'right' is likely to report high satisfaction with the performance of the state. At the same time, a civil servant who is well paid to do very little is less likely to want to accept bribes. In this way, Qatar's wealth has helped eliminate bribes in the public sector, while working to keep Qatar's neo-patrimonial system by minimizing the economic motivation for seeking regime change or reform. At the same time, fear of deportation has prevented government officials who come from migrant communities from engaging in corruption (Freedom House 2003).

Although Sheikh Hamad bin Khalifa engaged in top-down reforms, those reforms have retained the absolute rule of the Emir. In 2000, Hamad established the Council of the Ruling Family, consisting of thirteen family members, but he has often bypassed this Council. In 2005, he implemented a new constitution, passed by popular referendum in 2003 with 96% approval, which calls for the establishment of a partially elected Advisory Council to pass legislation to replace the current Advisory Council whose members are appointed by the Emir. The current Council has existed since the rule of Sheikh Khalifa, but it has been mostly filled with members of Al Thani and close allies of the Emir, and its role is largely ceremonial, to be informed of policies by the Emir, rather than formulating policies. However, the 2005 Constitution gives the Emir the power of veto over the Council, and the choice of appointing one third of its 45 members. Although the Emir's veto can be overruled if rejected by two-thirds of the Council, the Constitution gives the Emir the power to suspend legislation. Article 67 of the Constitution also effectively gives the Emir absolute power (Fromherz 2012).

To date, there has not been an Advisory Council election in Qatar, despite repeated promises by Sheikh Hamad, the latest being saying that such elections would take place in 2013.

2. Governance regime mechanisms

The persistence of a neo-patrimonial governance regime in Qatar is due to two factors: abundant public resources and a traditional tribal society that has been appropriated by a monarch with control over public resources. The modern state of Qatar has only existed for a generation, and thus has not had enough time to see a reduction in primordial economic and social ties and a growth of modernist forms of governance (Rathmell and

Schulze 2000). The Emir of Qatar uses resources from the export of oil and gas to secure the loyalty of supporters both from within the Al Thani family and from other tribes, thereby reducing tribal pressure on the regime to change its modus operandi. The same mechanism applies to citizens at large, who are granted land and subsidized goods and services in return for their loyalty.

Traditionally, tribal societies in the Middle East partly rule on the basis of consultation (shura) both among tribes and within tribes. Hamad has co-opted the tribal system by institutionalizing hereditary rule within the Al Thani family, by putting in place a new constitution in 2003 that stipulates this (Crystal 2011). Article 9 states that the Emir only needs to 'consult' - not seek approval from - the family council when choosing his heir, thereby allowing the Emir to bypass the traditional system of leadership succession (Fromherz 2012).

Studies of patrimonial states show that personal and social connections, not bribes, are the main type of privileged allocation in such states (Mungiu-Pippidi 2011). Qatar is no exception. Informal networks and 'wasta' (social connections), mainly based on tribal lineage, dominate the functioning of Qatar's formal institutions (Fromherz 2012). Because informal networks are an integral part of Qatari society, they are not perceived negatively, but are taken as a given. The Qatar World Values Survey 2010 reveals that 29% of Qataris attribute success to luck and 'wasta' only, with a further 15% attributing it to mostly luck and 'wasta'. At the same time, 91% of respondents reported that they have complete trust in their families, followed by 43% in the case of people they know personally, and 35% in the case of neighbours, compared with only 8% in the case of people from other nationalities and 5% in the case of those from other religions (see SESRI 2010). In this sense, one can safely conclude that privileged allocation on the basis of social connections is not seen as corruption - corruption is generally viewed as being about bribes, which is not a problem that Qatar suffers from in general.

3. Governance regime trends

The type of governance regime in Qatar has been consistent over time. However, the tipping point came with the takeover by Hamad bin Khalifa. Hamad's father had handed his son the task of modernizing the economy in Qatar, while Khalifa himself was extracting money from the Qatari state and not firmly pushing for economic progress. Hamad's bloodless coup was partly motivated by his frustration with the trajectory of economic development that Qatar had been following, and his recognition of untapped potential for the country's economic and political future (Kamrava 2009). Hamad worked on liberalizing the state and installing some top-down reforms, such as granting women suffrage and holding regular municipal elections, which first took place in 1999 and saw the participation of female candidates (Barany 2013). Hamad also abolished the Ministry of Information and gave the press more freedom. The establishment of Al-Jazeera in 1996 was a landmark for the Arab world, as it was the first pan-Arab channel engaged in open criticism of Arab governments and leaders - albeit never in the case of Qatari affairs.

The political openings installed by Sheikh Hamad are more to do with establishing legitimacy for the regime-and thus, continuity - than with the desire for genuine political reform. They are also driven by the Emir's political ambitions to put Qatar on the map in international relations and economic affairs. In order to be taken seriously by the international community, Qatar needs to cultivate an image of 'playing by the rules'. This approach paid off, resulting in the formation of alliances between the state of Qatar and key actors in the international community from across the political spectrum. Hamad, and his Prime Minister Hamad bin Jassim, established cordial relations with other states and non-state actors and used this to situate Qatar as a mediator in a number of conflicts in the Middle East, as well as an interlocutor with certain Islamist groups and regimes, like Hamas, the Muslim Brotherhood, and the Taliban. They also nurtured strong security alliances between Qatar and the United States, with Doha's hosting of US Central Command (Khatib 2013). On the domestic front, Hamad's reforms served to placate the limited demands for elections and freedom for the press that had been presented to his father in 1991 in a petition signed by a group of 54 prominent Qataris. Yet with the new Constitution cementing the rule of Al Thani, 'what the ruling elite are doing is increasing its legitimacy without jeopardizing its traditional position' (Ehteshami and Wright 2007, p. 922).

On the economic front, Sheikh Hamad directed a process of privatization that has sharply increased Qatar's international standing. In July 1995, the Doha Stock Market was established. Transparency and accountability measures to control business practices were introduced in both the public and private sectors (Crystal 2011). Those measures played a major role in controlling corruption: In 1970, 33% of total government expenditure was spent on the royal family, and throughout the 1980s, princes regularly extracted money from the Treasury for deposit in their personal Swiss bank accounts (Fromherz 2012). This practice was put under control by Sheikh Hamad, who recalibrated the informal state distribution mechanism by creating formal channels for monetary hand-outs in the shape of welfare (including property rights), subsidies, and employment. In this sense, Hamad's reforms can be seen as following the institutional evolution in which the state replaces feudal owners and distributes wealth to elites, thereby increasing the number of the privileged, and paving the way for later wider distribution (North and Weingast 1989).

Hamad also implemented reforms that ease doing business, including simplifying government administrative procedures to increase compliance with those procedures (including financial auditing and reporting); reducing the time needed for businesses to prepare for paying taxes; providing clear access to information about government regulations about the business sector; and making customs procedures for the import and export of goods more efficient - all resulting in high scores for Qatar on those fronts in international anti-corruption indices like the Global Competitiveness Index (GCI). The economic reforms paid off. Between July 2006 and November 2010, Qatar's rank in the GCI rose from 38 to 17. Foreign Direct Investment (FDI) has also risen, from 251 million dollars in 2000 to 8,722 million in 2009, indicating an opening up of the economy that has made it more attractive to foreign investors (Hvidt 2011). Foreign investment is seeing most growth in the sectors of oil, infrastructure (including construction), and financial services. Qatar has supported this by offering several incentives to foreign businesses, from facilitating the process of obtaining loans from the Qatar Development Bank to imposing zero taxes on exports to having no restrictions on overseas profit transfer. One consequence of the reforms is that the shadow economy only forms 18% of the size of GDP, which is significantly lower than the regional average of 27.08% of GDP (Schneider et al. 2010). Yet as Peterson argues, although economic reforms and initiatives in Gulf countries technically create private enterprises, 'their conception, planning, construction, and shepherding into operation remain supervised by the state' (Peterson 2009, p. 17).

Political and economic reforms have served to assure the continuity and stability of Qatar's economic standing and of its governance regime. Although Sheikh Hamad was the target of a political coup in 1996, he has succeeded in passing leadership to his son who appears to want to retain the direction taken by his father and to continue expanding Qatar's international economic footprint. Over the past five years, Qatar has been pursuing an expansive foreign investment process, buying major businesses, sports clubs, and buildings around the world and especially in Europe. It has succeeded in its bid to host the World Cup in 2022 despite several rumours about corruption plaguing the process. And it has an ambitious plan to extend a gas pipeline through Egypt and into the Levant.

On the one hand, the regime is likely to stay stable because of the lack of internal political dissent and the constant flow of wealth to citizens and tribal leaders. The previous Emir Hamad and his wife Sheikha Moza cultivated cult statuses for themselves as icons of modernity. The Qatar Foundation headed by Sheikha Moza has funded numerous education and social initiatives both within Qatar and in the Arab world, such as Doha's Education City, which has attracted major Western universities - mainly American - to open branches in the country. Education City is popular with the young Qatari generation, which regards this international presence with a sense of national pride. The small number and general homogeneity of Qatari citizens have also helped the Emir in running the country and directing its policies. The Arab revolutions that started in 2011 have not resulted in demands for reform in Qatar, despite Qatar's own support of the uprisings in places like Syria and Libya. As the countries in transition began to face serious political, economic, and security challenges and regressions, Gulf citizens at large (with the exception of oppositions in Bahrain, Yemen, and Saudi Arabia) have rallied around their governments, preferring stability over political change. This represents a continuation of public opinion before the Arab Spring: The Qatar World Values Survey 2010 revealed that 62% of Qataris said that maintaining order and stability is their individual priority, while only 11% said their priority is 'giving people more say in important government decisions' and 6% chose 'protecting freedom of speech' as a top priority (see SESRI 2010). Moreover, Qatar Value Surveys show that 75% and 74% of survey respondents selected the police and armed forces respectively as the state institutions they have most confidence in, followed by the judiciary (67%), 'parliament' (the unelected Advisory Council) (57%), and government institutions (52%). Gulf governments have in turn actively averted the potential for public action by increasing monetary hand-outs. In Qatar, the government increased public sector salaries by 60% in September 2011 in a pre-emptive measure against dissent (Toumi 2011). Sheikh Hamad was also careful not to alienate the tribes through the process of economic liberalization. By making tribes beneficiaries of economic reforms (such as by granting them high-profile positions - most companies in Qatar have a Qatari figurehead at the top of the senior management), this engagement has served to push the tribes into accepting Western institutions and standards, while also remaining loyal to the regime (Fromherz 2012). In addition, the international community's political and security interests have diverted attention away from Qatar's political and economic shortcomings as Qatar is seen as a key strategic ally for the West.

On the other hand, international attention to human rights infringements in Qatar is putting some pressure on the regime to reform, as seen in the cases of Mohamad al-Ajami, the Qatari poet imprisoned in 2012 for composing a poem seen as critical of the Emir, and the World Cup construction workers facing death and injuries caused by their working conditions (Franks 2013). Politically, Qatar's support for Islamist groups across the Middle East and North Africa has meant engaging with volatile political and paramilitary actors whose loyalty cannot be guaranteed in the long run, forming a potential source of instability for Qatar. Economic ambitions have also had an inadvertently negative impact on foreign policy, as illustrated by the case of the Muslim Brotherhood, with which Qatar has had a close relationship for decades. Qatar's plan to extend a gas pipeline to the Levant through Egypt was one reason behind support for its Muslim Brotherhood allies in Egypt and Syria, only for the Brotherhood leadership to be overthrown in Egypt and to be replaced in the National Coalition for Syrian Revolutionary and Opposition Forces. However, Qatar pursues a pragmatic foreign policy and has begun engaging with the new leaders in both countries to ensure its stability and economic interests. Alliances with Western countries also continue to support its regime stability. Domestically, the new generation of educated Qataris may, in the long run, not remain satisfied with its system of governance. Increased engagement with the international economy is also driving further economic reforms. But demand for and prospects of change in Qatar are not likely to emerge in the near future.

4. Corruption indicators and the governance regime

4.1. Power distribution

Power in Qatar is distributed in a top-down manner, i.e. by the Emir, who allocates key government, civil service and private company positions to members of his family and to tribal figures. Under Sheikh Hamad bin Khalifa, the Prime Minister—Hamad bin Jassim—was a cousin from the Al Thani family. Seven of the 19 key ministers were from the Al Thani family as well, as are the governor of the Central Bank and the current director of Al-Jazeera. Members of the family of Sheikha Moza, Al Missned, occupy key security positions, as do members of the family of the mother of Sheikh Hamad, Al Attiyah (The Economist 2010).

Qatar has a centralized local governance structure. As Jill Crystal explains, 'Qatar is divided administratively into ten municipalities (baladiyat). However since the majority of the population lives in the capital, local government is of little practical importance' (Crystal 2011, p. 183). Centralization and top-down control, coupled with the disempowerment of sources of discontent, and the lack of government elections, serve to keep the distribution of power in Qatar consistent.

4.2. State autonomy from private interest

In Qatar, there is no real separation between the state and the private interests of the ruling family. There are no lobbies, no government watchdogs, no independent civil society, and the freedom of the press is restricted when it comes to addressing internal affairs. Instead, citizens air their grievances through a traditional 'majlis' with tribal leaders, where people can submit petitions (The Economist 2010). Fromherz (2012) quotes Jill Crystal's statement about Qatar under Sheikh Khalifa as being still relevant today: 'power remains uninstitutionalized. There is no meaningful distinction, either political or legal, between the person of the Emir and the institutions of the state' (p. 125).

There is also no transparency in public procurement. There is an official procurement process in place as well as regulations regarding conflicts of interest; however, foreign companies have reported vagueness in the actual implementation of the process. The Global Integrity 2009 report additionally states that 'Public officials are not subject to financial disclosure laws and the State Audit Bureau is not mandated to audit the assets of these officials'. Another concern is that Articles 6 and 7 of Law 26 of 2005 regulating Tenders and Auctions 'permit tenders to bypass the public and competitive procurement process under specific circumstances; e.g., should there be an 'urgency in the need for the tender' or if there is a direct agreement established between the Central Tenders Committee and the company in light of the latter's rare products, works or services'. The Business Anti-corruption Portal adds that 'Unsuccessful bidders cannot challenge procurement decisions in court and companies found guilty of major procurement violations are not formally blacklisted. Several sources report that it often requires Qatar intermediaries or agents with good political connections to bid on large government contracts… Suppliers that use goods with Qatari content in their bids for government procurement enjoy preferential treatment as the government offers them a 10% discount on these goods' (Business Anti-corruption Portal 2013). In this sense, informal networks overrule regulations.

4.3. Public allocation

Public allocation in Qatar follows a rentier system. State wealth is subject to distribution, with the existence of a welfare state that increases dependence on foreign expatriates to be the real work force, while Qatari nationals take state distributions for granted (Peterson 2009). While non-citizens pay for health care, electricity, water, and education, those services, in addition to housing, are provided to citizens for free (US Department of State 2011). Fuel is subsidized for businesses as well as citizens, and Qatari businesses and agriculture also receive capital, electricity, and water subsidies (Losman 2010).

The current Emir, Sheikh Tamim, is the head of the board of directors of the QIA responsible for domestic and foreign investments. The previous Prime Minister and Minister of Foreign Affairs, Hamad bin Jassim Al Thani, was also vice-chairman and CEO of the QIA while he was in office, and has now been replaced with the Emir's half-brother Sheikh Abdullah bin Hamad Al Thani (Middle East Online 2013). The QIA does not publish its holdings, making it unclear whether it handles royal investments or not. In this way, the state is not autonomous from private interests. It is difficult to establish the extent of this due to the lack of public information.

4.4. Relation between formal and informal institutions

Qatar's formal institutions intermingle with informal ones, mainly tribes. A major challenge for formal institutions in Qatar is that they are not always taken seriously because they are subverted by informal institutions. As The Economist reports, in the municipal elections in 1999, 'turnout for registration was so low that the government had to extend the deadline by a week to rustle up voters.… Most of Qatar's leading families did not take the poll seriously enough to field any candidates of their own' (The Economist 1999b). Among those who voted, almost all respondents in a survey conducted shortly after the elections revealed that they did so mainly according to tribal affiliations. The current appointed Advisory Council is dominated by Al Thani family members and tribal representatives, which are used by the Emir to ensure their consensus (Fromherz 2012).

4.5. Accountability and rule of law

Part of Sheikh Hamad's reforms covered the judiciary. In 1999, a court of final appeal was added to the Qatari legal system (Rathmell and Schulze 2000), following the establishment of the High Judicial Council 'tasked with offering advice on judicial appointments and to propose legislation concerning the judicial system. In October 2004, long-promised court reform unified Qatar's dual court system (of Shari'a and civil courts). In 2007 an Administrative Court and a Constitutional Court were established' (Crystal 2011, p. 185). In 2008, a Supreme Court was added, although the Emir appoints all of its justices. Although the judiciary system has been perceived as efficient in its operations, it suffers from the same infrastructural problems as other state institutions. The Emir also appoints all judges, implying that Qatari judges are selected on the basis of social connections, while non-Qatari judges are vulnerable to deportation (see Heritage Foundation 2013). Thus, court cases involving foreign nationals frequently discriminate in favour of Qataris (Global Integrity Report 2009 in Langer 2009). Law enforcement authorities are also more likely to grant bail to citizens while noncitizens are more likely to be remanded to custody (US Department of State 2011).

Courts in Qatar do not engage in checks on the ruler. Court orders against royals and tribal allies are rare and have tended to revolve around failed coups, such as the case of the cousin of Sheikh Hamad who attempted a coup in 1996 and was arrested in 1999 (The Economist 1999a), and the case of Al Murrah tribe connected with the same coup, who were stripped of their Qatari nationality until it was restored in 2006 (Crystal 2011). An exceptional case is that of Sheikh Ali bin Jassim Al Thani, who was sentenced to six years in prison for involuntary manslaughter in 2013 following a fire that erupted at the Villaggio shopping centre the year before. However, Ali and the other three defendants are currently out of jail awaiting appeal (Doha News 2013). Normally, corrupt practices by princes are settled out of court as princes are granted immunity. Two examples are Sheikh Khalifa's departure with billions from Treasury money in 1995, and Hamad bin Jassim's alleged involvement in an arms deal in 1998, in which BAE paid bin Jassim £7 million in 'commission' for arranging the deal. Investigation of the deal was halted due to pressure on Britain by Qatar and BAE and the case was settled out of court (The Guardian 2007).

Qatari state institutions may engage in good practices but they do not have transparent infrastructures: State Audit Bureau reports are not made public and the head of the Bureau is appointed by the Emir. The National Human Rights Committee has limited ability and refrains from reporting on corruption cases. The National Committee for Accountability and Transparency, established in 2007, does not have public information or contact details. 'Evaluations regarding the performance of the Committee are mixed with the US Department of State 2010 noting that it carries out its mandate well and is regarded as effective, while it its performance is considered as "weak" by Global Integrity 2009, mainly due to high political interference in its affairs' (see Heritage Foundation 2013). A new organization was established in 2011, called the Administrative Control and Transparency Authority. Its mandate includes 'probing the misuse of public funds and investigating complaints against government officials'. However, the Authority also does not publish public information. Qatari law additionally does not provide public access to government information, 'such as the budget, expenditures, or draft laws' (US Department of State 2013).

4.6. Personal autonomy and collective action capacity

Qatar's wealth has contributed to sustaining a sense of political apathy by negating the drive for economic-based calls for political change (Ulrichsen 2011). From the distractions offered by investments in sports and clubs to public sector employment, public services, and distributions based on social connections, the country's economy has served to stifle interest in political participation. The Qatar World Values Survey 2010 shows that 64% of Qataris named economic growth as their highest priority for Qatar, with only 16% saying their top national priority is more participation in decision making in work and community matters, despite 69% of all respondents saying that they either 'very interested' (15%) or 'somewhat interested' (54%) in politics (see SESRI 2010).

Interest in politics does not necessarily mean interest in engaging in political activities, and this is not helped by the state of political parties and civil society: the former are banned, and the latter is not independent and is reliant on state revenue (Fromherz 2012). All nongovernmental associations - private, professional, and cultural - must be registered with and are monitored by the state (Blanchard 2008), 'and most groups… have had license requests refused' (Crystal 2011, p. 183). Justin Gengler and Mark Tessler's analysis of Qatar World Values Survey 2010 results regarding civic life also reveals that 'Qataris who channel their social, economic, and political ambitions through participation in civic associations are disproportionately likely to be less tolerant of others, less oriented towards democracy, and less confident in formal governmental institutions' (2011, p. 3). As the authors explain, Qataris 'seem to engage in association life primarily in order to seek their private advantage and interact with like-minded individuals, ends that serve exactly to reinforce rather than challenge the established social and political system' (Gengler and Tessler 2011, p. 13).

Crystal (2011) explains, 'In 2004 the government did issue a new labour law, giving Qataris the right to form trade unions and engage in collective bargaining (including the right to strike)' (p. 183). But The General Union of Workers of Qatar has a limited scope of action and is forbidden from affiliating with groups outside the country. Labour laws also offer little protection to non-citizens, as there is no minimum wage and employment for foreigners in Qatar is dependent on getting sponsorship from a Qatari national. This system has opened up the doors for human rights abuses, as illustrated in the case of Nepalese workers constructing World Cup sites, and whose abysmal working conditions have been linked with a high rate of deaths in their ranks. The sponsorship system is also open to abuse by mediators who recruit foreign nationals on commission, or who manipulate the law to take advantage of vulnerable foreign workers. Global Integrity has reported in 2009 that there have been cover-ups of incidents of worker abuse in order to maintain a good image of Qatar abroad and of influential families. The US State Department also reports in 2011:

> expats are ineligible to form worker committees and can only be members of joint labor-management committees. Government employees cannot join the union. There are strict conditions on workers' strikes, making such collective action unlikely. A strike must be approved by ¾ of the company's workers committee, and the Labor Department must rule on all industrial disputes before a strike may be called. On 23 September 2010, 90 expat laborers began a strike protesting a 35% pay cut in violation of their contracts. All strike participants were arrested and deported. Those employees who had worked less than two years for the company in question, al-Badar Construction, were required to pay for their return tickets home.

At the same time, 'The right to peaceful public assembly is restricted. Public demonstrations… are banned. Permission is still required for public gatherings and demonstrations, and the government grants these reluctantly' (Crystal 2011, p. 183). Among the migrant communities, demands for reform or participation in protests are therefore rare as foreign workers are concerned about retaining their residency and jobs (Barany 2013). Although Al Jazeera has gained a reputation as a daring news outlet, Qatari law restricts press freedom. For example, the 2002 media law states that journalists can be punished for 'criticizing friendly governments' (Barany 2013, p. 28). Despite the lifting of formal censorship in 1995, self-censorship in the media is regular practice. Al Jazeera refrains from criticizing Qatari affairs, and has since 2011 been put under the directorship of a member of Al Thani (Crystal 2011). While the seven daily newspapers in Qatar are not state owned, they are owned by members of the royal family or have close ties to the government. Foreign newspapers and magazines brought into Qatar are subject to censorship, as is internet usage for political and religious content (US Department of State 2011).

There are also indirect restrictions on reporting on corruption due to social conditions and the absence of a legal framework that can enable this reporting. According to Global Integrity 2009, the civil service has experienced an increasing independence since the government introduced a law in 2007 providing civil sector employees with the possibility to bring their grievances to court. The new law regulates the Administrative Court to resolve disputes between government bodies and citizens. Nevertheless, the report notes that very few would file complaints as undefined barriers built by societal stigmas impose self-censorship on public sector employees; these include reporting on corruption or inefficiencies.

There are no laws to protect whistle blowers, no anti-corruption watchdog, and no non-governmental anti-corruption initiatives, since Law 12 of 2004 makes it illegal for civil society organizations to focus on fighting corruption (see Business Anti-Corruption Portal 2013).

Summary and conclusions

The governance regime in Qatar is a solid neo-patrimonial, particularist one that places citizens as clients in a rentier state. As such, Qatar's system can be described as falling under the 'official moguls' label in Michael Johnston's typology of corruption. Johnson writes that in countries labelled as such, 'institutions are very weak, politics remains undemocratic or is opening up only slowly, but the economy is being liberalized at least to a degree. Civil society is weak or non-existent. Opportunities for enrichment and new risks for the already wealthy abound - but political power is personal, and is often used with impunity' (Johnston 2005, p. 46). Centralization of power and top-down control, coupled with the disempowerment of sources of discontent, and the lack of government elections, serve to keep the distribution of power in Qatar consistent. However, unlike the case of most neo-patrimonial states, Qatari citizens report a high degree of satisfaction and quality of life, driven by the state's support of most of their economic needs. Citizens appear to have comfort, but little personal or collective agency. Another particularity is that despite the co-optation of the tribal system, tribes do constitute a form of checking on the Emir's authority, whose desire for political stability drives him to keep the tribes satisfied.

Informal networks, mainly based on tribal relations, permeate state institutions and associational life. Public procurement is not transparent and is reliant on social connections. But there are no mechanisms to prevent this as accountability and the rule of law are mostly dependent on who is the point of focus: The ruling family is above the law, as there are no accountability procedures, neither political (no elections) nor economic that apply to it. Public information about state institutions, including anti-corruption organizations, is largely absent, and the media refrain from reporting on corruption due to self-censorship as well as to their close ties to the government. Meanwhile, civil society organizations are prevented from engaging in anti-corruption activities, while they are themselves not independent from the state. Citizens are disempowered and lack interest in political participation, and state hand-outs ensure they refrain from voicing demands for reform. Migrants, on the other hand, are too scared to speak up about corruption or human rights abuses due to their complete dependence on Qatari job sponsorship. The Qatari judiciary may operate efficiently, but judges discriminate against foreigners and judges are not fully independent, as they are appointed by the Emir. Western countries have been largely silent about the shortcomings of the governance regime in Qatar because of their political, economic, and security interests that are invested in the regime and its stability.

Despite those factors, Qatar has engaged in more reforms to fight corruption than other countries in the Middle East and North Africa, and its success can be attributed to making economic bureaucracies efficient, eliminating the temptation to engage in petty corruption. Its liberalization of the economy has also forced it to adhere to international standards in order to attract foreign investors and traders. There has been a move to better governance in Qatar as demonstrated by the Emir's control of access to Treasury money by the royal family, the facilitations offered to businesses, and the increased exposure to global markets with strict anti-corruption requirements, which has forced Qatar to adhere to certain international standards. However, the reforms remain strictly top-down measures directed by the government, and exclude the ruling family and people in the business community with close ties to the government. As such, no matter the position of Qatar in anti-corruption indicators, 'good governance' in Qatar remains partial, not universal. In addition, good governance is about more than anti-corruption measures alone, and the principles of good governance (transparency, accountability, equality, etc.) are largely missing in Qatar. Although Qatar has the potential to evolve into having an open economic system, this transformation is constrained by its political and social milieu. Only when meaningful political reform and social change occur in Qatar can the country be seen as able to formulate comprehensive anti-corruption policies that are implemented transparently.

Methodological implications for anti-corruption measurement

There are four main lessons that can be drawn from this study. First, an examination of the structures and mechanisms of the governance regime in Qatar is needed to reveal the complexities and contradictions that seem to be missed by international anti-corruption indices. Such indices focus on what is known and on actors within the law, but it is difficult to objectively measure performances and practices of entities that place themselves above the law. The high level of legal cases settled out of court for example hides the real degree of engagement in corruption by members of the royal family, and that is not to mention the incidents of corruption that never make it to court due to personal and social connections and institutionalized favouritism.

Second, the analysis in this case study suggests that the methodology used in the corruption indices is likely to have a biased impact on scores. Transparency International's CPI, the WGI, and the GCI - which have rated Qatar highly in terms of anti-corruption measures - all partially rely on surveys or interviews with respondents from the resident business community who are asked about their perceptions rather than about in-country practices. The WGI also includes subjective assessments from non-governmental organizations and public sector bodies. However, as this study has shown, in the case of Qatar, the former are not independent from government influence and the latter are controlled by the ruling family. Qataris are bound by social ties and concerns about security and stability and foreign residents live in fear of deportation for speaking up, in the absence of laws that guarantee their human rights. The three indices' focus on respondents from the economic sector, which has been bureaucratized effectively, has also meant overlooking corruption within the political system.

As such, the context in which information for those three indices is gathered casts a shadow of doubt over the validity of the scores. A case in point is revealed by looking at measures of independence of the judiciary as revealed by those indicators, compared with results from the Human Rights Dataset, which relies on Amnesty International reports and the State Department's Country Reports on Human Practices - i.e., indicators of practice rather than perception - as sources.

Third, the analysis reveals that the specific indicators conventionally used to measure anti-corruption are incomplete, due to nuances not covered by those indicators. In their approach to what constitutes corruption, anti-corruption indices focus on bribery but miss measuring social allocation. Therefore, particular questions need to be asked to get a fuller picture of corruption and anti-corruption in Qatar, although answers to those questions are difficult to obtain because of Qatar's opaque governance system. Those questions include:

1. Is there public information about public expenditure? How transparent is public procurement? Unfortunately, there is little public information about this issue beyond anecdotal evidence.
2. Where do sources of information on corruption come from? Is there a freedom of information act? In the case of Qatar, information mostly comes from the government and the media are not free to report on corruption.

3. Where do anti-corruption initiatives come from? Are there any non-governmental anti-corruption initiatives? In the case of Qatar, all initiatives come from the government, which suggests lack of validity.
4. Is there a monitoring and accountability framework so that people know what is going on in their government? As Francis Fukuyama has argued, if one cannot measure, one cannot hold the government accountable, but it is often hard to measure the performance of government services (Fukuyama 2004). In Qatar, there is no watchdog to measure government performance and hold it accountable.
5. How independent is civil society? In Qatar, civil society is not independent.
6. How is corruption defined? In Qatar, corruption seems to be narrowly defined as being about bribes, while social connections linked with privileged allocation are widely accepted.

Finally, current governance indicators focus on measures related to the scope of state functions, but they miss measuring the strength of state institutions and state capacity. Fukuyama defines the scope of state activity as the different functions of the state, and state institution strength as the 'ability of states to plan and execute policies, and to enforce laws cleanly and transparently' (Fukuyama 2004, p. 22). He argues that in order to implement measures like business regulation, functioning court systems, and service delivery, states need to have capacity, such as the availability of money, people, education, and an efficient organizational culture. Within the latter, he points out that policymakers should be separate from policy implementers. As this analysis has revealed, while the Qatari state has the wealth and the bureaucracy, it lacks the human capacity and instead relies on foreign workers who work under great constraints, in addition to not investing in an indigenous highly skilled work force, and to having an organizational culture dominated by the ruling family and permeated by informal networks at all levels. Qatar's state institutions may appear strong (and have indeed often been characterized as such) because of certain bureaucracies in place, but they lack important components of state capacity. The indicators therefore miss the weakness of Qatar's state institutions, and therefore the 'missing link' between Qatar's high ranking regarding anti-corruption and the context of its governance regime.

References

Amnesty International (2013) 'Qatar: The dark side of migration: Spotlight on Qatar's construction sector ahead of the World Cup', 18 November 2013. Available from: <http://www.amnesty.org/en/library/info/MDE22/010/2013/en>

Barany, Z. (2013) 'Unrest and State Response in Arab Monarchies', *Mediterranean Quarterly*, 24(20), pp. 5-38

Berrebi, C., Martorell, F. and Tanner, J. C. (2009) 'Qatar's Labor Markets at a Crucial Crossroad', *The Middle East Journal* 63(3), pp. 421-42

Blanchard, C. M. (2008) 'Qatar: Background and US Relations'. Congressional Research Service. Available from: <http://wlstorage.net/file/crs/RL31718.pdf>

Business Anti-corruption Portal (2013) Qatar Country Profile. Available from: <http://www.business-anti-corruption.com/country-profiles/middle-east-north-africa/qatar/snapshot.aspx>

Crystal, J. (2011) 'Eastern Arabian States: Kuwait, Bahrain, Qatar, United Arab Emirates and Oman'. In D. E. Long et al. (eds.), *The Government and Politics of the Middle East and North Africa*, pp. 161-204

Doha News (2013) 'Five charged in Villaggio fire deaths sentenced to jail for involuntary manslaughter', June 20. Available from: <http://dohanews.co/five-villaggio-trial-defendants-jailed-for-involuntary/>

Ehteshami, A. and Wright, S. (2007) 'Political change in the Arab oil monarchies: from liberalization to enfranchisement'. *International Affairs* 83(5), pp. 913-32

Franks, T. (2013) 'Sporting events shine spotlight on Qatar's human rights'. *BBC News*, 25 Jan 2013. Available from: <http://www.bbc.co.uk/news/world-middle-east-21202067>

Freedom House (2003) *Freedom in the World 2003*. Available from: <http://www.freedomhouse.org/report/freedom-world/freedom-world-2003>

Freedom House (2010) *Freedom in the World 2010*. Available from: <http://www.freedomhouse.org/report/freedom-world/freedom-world-2010#.Uvd34_mSxrU>

Fromherz, A. J. (2012) *Qatar: A Modern History*. Washington, DC: Georgetown University Press

Fukuyama, F. (2004) 'The Imperative of State-Building' *Journal of Democracy* 15(2), pp. 17-31

Gengler, J. and Tessler, M. (2011) 'Civic Life and Democratic Citizenship in Qatar: Findings from the First Qatar World Values Survey', Middle East Law and Governance, 5(3), pp. 258-79

Heritage Foundation (2013) *Index of Economic Freedom – Qatar*. Available from: <http://www.heritage.org/index/country/qatar>

Human Rights Dataset (2010) Available from: <http://www.humanrightsdata.org/>

Hvidt, M. (2011) 'Economic and Institutional Reforms in the Arab Gulf States', *The Middle East Journal* 65(1), pp. 85-102

Johnston, M. (2005) *Syndromes of Corruption: Wealth, Power, and Democracy*. Cambridge: Cambridge University Press

Kamrava, M. (2009) 'Royal Factionalism and Political Liberalization in Qatar'. *The Middle East Journal* 63(3), pp. 401-20

Khatib, L. (2013) 'Qatar's Foreign Policy: The Limits of Pragmatism', *International Affairs* 89(2), pp. 417-31

Langer, N. (2009) Global Integrity Report 2009: Qatar, Available from: <http://report.globalintegrity.org/Qatar/2009/notebook>

Losman, D. L. (2010) 'The Rentier State and National Oil Companies: An Economic and Political Perspective', *The Middle East Journal* 64(3), pp. 427-45

Middle East Online (2013) 'No surprise as Qatar dismisses Hamad Bin Jassim from Investment Authority', 2 July. Available from: <http://www.middle-east-online.com/english/?id=59847>

Mungiu-Pippidi, A. (2006) 'Corruption: Diagnosis and Treatment', *Journal of Democracy*, 17(3), pp. 86–99

Mungiu-Pippidi, A. et al. (2011) Contextual Choices in Fighting Corruption: Lessons Learned, NORAD, Report 4/2011. Available from: <http://www.norad.no/en/tools-and-publications/publications/publication?key=383808>

North, D. C. and Weingast, B. R. (1989) 'Constitutions and Commitment: The Evolution of Institutions Governing Public Choice in Seventeenth-Century England', *The Journal of Economic History* 49(4), pp. 803-32

O'Donnell, G. (1996) 'Illusions about Consolidation', *Journal of Democracy* 7(2), pp. 34-51

Peterson, J. E. (2009) 'Life after Oil: Economic Alternatives for the Arab Gulf States', *Mediterranean Quarterly* 20(3), pp. 1-18

Rathmell, A., and Schulze, K. (2000) 'Political Reform in the Gulf: The Case of Qatar'. *Middle East Studies* 36(4), pp. 47-62

Schneider, F., Buehn, A. and Montenegro, C. E. (2010) 'Shadow Economies all over the World: New Estimates for 162 Countries from 1999 to 2007'. *The World Bank, Policy Research Working Paper Series no. 5356.* Available from: <http://ideas.repec.org/p/wbk/wbrwps/5356.html>

SESRI (Social and Economic Survey Research Institute) (2010) *Qatar World Values Survey 2010.* Available from: <http://xn--mgbeh7c1c.xn--wgbl6a/sesri/documents/QWVS_English_press_release__Final.pdf>

The Economist, (1999a) 'Royal jigsaw in Qatar', 29 July 1999. Available from: <http://www.economist.com/node/228095>

The Economist, (1999b) 'Voting Fun', 11 May 1999. Available from: <http://www.economist.com/node/319329>

The Economist, (2010) 'Qatar and its emir: He'll do it his way', 27 May 2010. Available from: <http://www.economist.com/node/16219226>

The Guardian (2007) 'The BAE Files', 7 June 2007. Available from: <http://www.theguardian.com/world/2007/jun/07/bae2>

Toumi, H. (2011) 'Public sector in Qatar to get 60 per cent pay rise', *Gulf News*, 7 September 2011. Available from: <http://gulfnews.com/news/gulf/qatar/public-sector-in-qatar-to-get-60-per-cent-pay-rise-1.862595>

Transparency International (2011) 'Corruption Perception Index 2011: A short methodological note'. Available from: <http://www.transparency.de/Methodologische-Hinweise.2018.0.html> [in German]

Transparency International (2012) *Corruption Perception Index 2012.* Available from: <http://cpi.transparency.org/cpi2012/results/>

Ulrichsen, K. C. (2011) 'Qatar and the Arab Spring', *Open Democracy*, 12 April 2011. Available from: <http://www.opendemocracy.net/kristian-coates-ulrichsen/qatar-and-arab-spring>

US Department of State (2011) '2010 Human Rights Report: Qatar'. Available from: <http://www.state.gov/j/drl/rls/hrrpt/2010/nea/154471.htm>

US Department of State, (2013) '2012 Human Rights Report: Qatar'. Available from: <http://www.state.gov/documents/organization/204590.pdf>

World Bank (2010) *Worldwide Governance Indicators 2010.* Available from: <http://info.worldbank.org/governance/wgi/index.aspx#reports>

Yom, S. L., and Gause F. G. (2012). 'Resilient Royals: How Arab Monarchies Hang On', *Journal of Democracy* 23(4), pp. 74-88

5. Are EU funds a Corruption Risk? The Impact of EU Funds on Grand Corruption in Central and Eastern Europe

MIHÁLY FAZEKAS, JANA GUTIERRÉZ CHVALKOVSKÁ, JIŘÍ SKUHROVEC, ISTVÁN JÁNOS TÓTH AND LAWRENCE PETER KING

It is hard to miss the 'buzz' around how extensively corruption affects the spending of European Union (EU) funds across many new and old member states: Italian mafia hijacking highway projects, or the European Commission freezing Structural Funds payments in countries such as Romania, Bulgaria, or Hungary. Some of these cases point at the involvement of high-level politics and organised criminal groups, raising the possibility that the EU in fact extensively finances large-scale corruption in a number of countries. EU funds constitute a considerable part of GDP in many member states, especially in Central and Eastern Europe (CEE) where it amounts to 1.9-4.4% of annual member state GDPs (KPMG 2012) and well above 50% of public investment. Even if only a fraction of these amounts is impacted by corruption, the negative effects are likely to be considerable in terms of misinvestment and distorted economic incentives, jeopardizing regional convergence. If corruption in EU funds spending is connected to high-level politics and organised crime, ramifications are more severe, impacting political competition, democracy, and eventually social welfare.

Given high level of perception of corruption risks in EU funds spending, especially in CEE, the large sums involved, and the potential negative consequences, this chapter sets out to explore **the impact of EU funds spending on institutionalised grand corruption in CEE.**

It focuses on three new EU member states: **Czech Republic, Hungary, and Slovakia** throughout 2009-12. These three EU member states represent different levels of wealth and development trajectories. Their political institutions differ considerably with Hungary lately displaying increasingly authoritarian characteristics and generally failing to tackle corruption; Slovakia making some progress towards clean government albeit with question marks, and Czech Republic being one of the good performers of CEE while displaying some signs of a deteriorating situation. In spite of differences, these countries share a broadly similar post-communist heritage and a relatively homogenous regulatory framework defined by the EU.

2009-12 constitutes a turbulent period with the global economic crisis unfolding and turning into a sovereign debt crisis in Europe, with the three countries being affected in different ways. There was at least one general election in 2009-12 in each of these countries. This turbulent environment provides the perfect setting for testing the robustness of our theory in different political and economic contexts.

EU funds are spent in various forms, which makes it impossible to arrive at a blanket assessment. Therefore, this analysis only looks at **public procurement spending by public or semi-public organisations (e.g. state owned enterprises) financed from EU funds**, which predominantly means the use of Cohesion and Structural Funds. The advantage of this approach is that we can compare projects which are similar in most respects apart from the source of financing. Moreover, there is exceptionally good data available on public procurement spending in all three countries on the level of individual contracts for the period. Our approach is a major departure from prior studies in this area, as it utilizes a large-scale micro-level quantitative database, which allows for unearthing a rich detailed picture on the level of individual actors while also being broad enough to evaluate whole systems of governance.

1. Previous work

In spite of the considerable public and policy interest in corruption risks in EU funds spending, there is **remarkably little scientific work on the question to date.** Looking into the broader discussion, there are two potential sources of theoretical underpinning: the broad economic, sociological, and political science literature on aid dependence and the Europeanization literature in political science. These offer no unambiguous theoretical expectation on whether and how EU funds contribute to the quality of institutions and impact corruption. Rather, what we find is a set of conflicting predictions and mechanisms which need empirical evaluation.

The literature looking at the effect of development aid on quality of institutions and corruption is vast; however, it can be applied to the context of CEE countries and EU funds only with caution due to the differing contexts and funding volumes (i.e. EU funding amounts to 3-4% of recipient countries' GDP whereas many developing countries receive aid more than 10% of GDP). Nevertheless, according to this literature, **foreign aid can have a positive effect on governance** by providing clear policy goals of improving the civil service and helping countries to overcome the lack of resources for state building (Knack 2001). However, **development aid can also destroy institutions** and impede state building in a similar way as natural resources can (Djankov, Montalvo and Reynal-Querol 2008). Development aid can weaken accountability and the development of civil society by breaking the link between domestic revenues (i.e. taxation) and government services. It can also directly destruct domestic administrative capacity by reallocating talented bureaucrats from domestic institutions to aid organisations and by providing additional organisational goals potentially increasing institutional fragmentation. Probably most importantly, development aid increases the pool of public resources available for rent seeking which can mean more corruption in countries with low control of it (Bräutigam 2000). While these causal pathways may work differently in the CEE context, the above arguments may still account for a large part of the mechanisms linking EU funds to corruption in the region. Combining these insights with scholarship specific to CEE and EU governance leads to more robust theoretical underpinnings.

In the literature on the process of Europeanization, few would debate that the **EU contributed to institution building and improvement of governance in CEE countries throughout the accession process** (Epstein and Sedelmeier 2009). The EU provided the highly popular goal of accession for CEE governments and guidance on which institutional improvements should be implemented to reach this goal albeit with varying clarity (Meyer-Sahling 2011). These resulted in a wealth of reforms of public administration, democratic checks and balances, or financial management. However, many authors expressed **concerns that CEE countries reversed a range of reforms after accession** and left many EU-supported and/or requested new rules as 'empty shells' (Epstein and Sedelmeier 2009; Mungiu-Pippidi 2007). These concerns stem from the EU's diminishing leverage to keep new member states in line with principles of good government and the perception that many pre-accession reforms have not become embedded in domestic law or administrative activity. Many of these reforms were either 'implemented' only on paper or created islands of excellence isolated from the rest of public administration (Goetz 2001).

Similarly to the literature on aid dependency, the Europeanization literature delivers good reasons for believing that **EU funds advance good government**. First, one of the most important remaining post-accession tools in Brussels for disciplining new member states is the promise of allocating or the threat of withdrawing EU fund (Epstein and Sedelmeier 2009) which should motivate recipient countries to manage funds well. Second, the disbursement of EU funds is more heavily regulated, making corruption more costly. Heavy administrative and regulatory requirements can also contribute to higher administrative capacity in the recipient organisations as they often have to invest in their capacities to be able to receive and manage EU funds. Third, extensive monitoring and controls of EU funds in addition to the usual national audit frameworks make detection and punishment of corruption more likely (European Commission 2003; European Court of Auditors 2012, 2013). Moreover, the European Court of Justice represents an additional venue for judicial review, making the capture of domestic courts a less effective way of avoiding punishment for corruption.

Similar to the development aid literature, Europeanization literature also delivers arguments stating that external funding such as **EU funds in CEE deteriorate the quality of government and increase corruption** for at least three reasons. First, EU Cohesion and Structural Funds are spent on investment projects where public discretion is high. From the wider literature, it is clear that discretionary spending is more likely to involve corruption than non-discretionary spending such as pensions (Mauro 1998; Tanzi and Davoodi 2001). Second, EU funding provides a large additional pool of public resources for rent extraction. Hence, all else being equal, EU funds add to the pool of particularistically allocated public resources (Mungiu-Pippidi 2013). Third, EU funds, like external funding in developing countries, weaken the link between domestic civil society, taxation, and policy performance.

In addition to the broader arguments above, preliminary evidence from Hungary (Fazekas, Tóth and King 2013c) and Romania (Dimulescu, Pop and Doroftei 2013) suggests that corruption in EU funds reaches up to high-level politicians. Therefore, it is conceivable that EU funds, in fact, fuel high-level corruption networks which can simultaneously control business and political positions. This implies that EU funding keeps corrupt elites in power rather than promoting integrity.

From the above discussion, the following hypotheses result:
on the one hand,

H0: EU funds decrease institutionalised grand corruption in CEE,

on the other hand:

HA: EU funds increase institutionalised grand corruption in CEE.

In the context of public procurement, institutionalised grand corruption refers to the allocation and performance of public procurement contracts by bending prior explicit rules and principles of good public procurement in order to benefit a closed network while denying access to all others (Mungiu-Pippidi 2006; North, Wallis and Weingast 2009; Rothstein and Teorell 2008).

While causal mechanisms cannot be tested one by one in detail, two major effects can be identified and hence will be tested separately: 1) the effect of additional resources represented by EU funding; and 2) the effect of different monitoring and incentive structures attached to EU funding.

2. Data and variables

2.1. Data sources

The database derives from public procurement announcements from 2009-12 in Czech Republic, Hungary, and Slovakia (this database is called the Public Procurement Comparative database, referred to as the **PPC** henceforth). The data represent a complete database of all public procurement procedures conducted under national public procurement laws. The PPC contains variables appearing in 1) calls for tenders, 2) contract award notices, 3) contract modification notices, and 4) administrative corrections notices. Not all announcements are available for every procedure, meaning that we have information on contract award notices for all procedures. All the countries' public procurement legislation is within the framework of the EU Public Procurement Directive and hence is, by and large, comparable. Utilization of certain regulatory tools is different, nevertheless, which provides useful variability for later analysis.

The data derives from official government online sources in each country (Table 1). As there is no readily available database, we used a crawler algorithm to capture every announcement available online. Then, applying a complex automatic and manual text mining strategy, we created a structured database, which contains variables with well-defined categories. As the original texts available online contain a range of errors, inconsistencies, and omissions, we applied several correction measures to arrive at a database of sufficient quality for scientific research[1]. For a full description of database development, see Soudek and Skuhrovec (2013) on the Czech Republic, Fazekas and Tóth (2012a, 2012b) on Hungary, and Transparency International Slovakia (2009) on Slovakia.

Table 1. Primary sources of public procurement data and minimum thresholds.

Country	Source of PPC data	URL	Minimum thresholds (EUR)[1]
Czech Republic	Ministerstvo pro místnírozvoj ČR	http://www.isvzus.cz/usisvz/	39,000
Hungary	KözbeszerzésiÉrtesítő	http://www.kozbeszerzes.hu/	27,300
Slovakia	Úrad pre verejnéobstarávanie	http://www.uvo.gov.sk/sk/evestnik	30,000

The resulting database describes at the micro-level a considerable proportion of GDPs and public spending in these three countries (**Table 2**). In spite of the relative similarity of thresholds for applying national public procurement laws, the three countries have very different proportions of transparent public procurement spending to total GDP. On the one hand, this is due to the use of exceptions, most notably in Hungary, and announcing contract awards in the official journal even if they would fall outside the remit of the law, most typically in the Czech Republic. On the other hand, this is due to the different total amounts spent on public procurement in the three countries whereby Hungary spends the least.

Table 2. Main statistics of the analysed data by country, total public procurement spending, 2009-2012.

	Czech Republic	Slovakia	Hungary	Total
Total number of contracts awarded (with valid contract value)	46945	20841	51231	119017
Total number of unique winners	11015	4912	10739	26666
Total number of unique issuers	5838	2069	5171	13078
Combined value of awarded contracts (million EUR)*	41591	22947	12514	77052
Combined value of awarded contracts (% GDP)**	6.90%	8.50%	3.20%	6.10%

Notes: * Exchanged into EUR using average monthly exchange rate of the contract award, not corrected for inflation; ** GDP figures are from Eurostat (GDP at market prices).
Source: PPC.

---

[1] For example, contract award announcements and calls for tenders are directly linked through a unique procedure ID in the Czech Republic only. Whereas in Hungary and Slovakia, the announcements refer to each other in varying formats making our linking procedure imperfect.

2.2. Variables used in the analysis

i. *EU funds use*

The spending of EU funds in public procurement can be directly identified in each contract award announcement which records the use or non-use of EU funds along with the reference to the corresponding EU program (this latter information will only be used at a later research stage as it requires text mining procedures for precise program identification). However, no information is published as to the proportion of EU funding within the total contract value. Hence, we had to employ a simplistic **yes-no categorisation of each contract awarded**. In most cases, regulation allows for the EU contribution to cover 80-95% of total investment. Data from large investment projects indicate that EU funds amount to the majority of project costs if EU funding is involved. Our approach nevertheless implies that throughout this paper, EU funding figures also include some national co-financing of between 5-20%.

Contrary to popular perceptions, public procurement from EU funds does not fall under a different procedural regime. The same procurement rules and thresholds apply regardless of funding source. **Common national and European public procurement legal frameworks warrant a meaningful comparison between EU funded and non-EU funded public procurement procedures**. The crucial difference between procurement procedures funded from EU funds and by national governments lies in additional monitoring and controls and different motivation structures associated with spending EU funds.

The three countries have made use of EU funding in their procurement spending to varying degrees with Hungary spending most extensively (**Figure 1**).

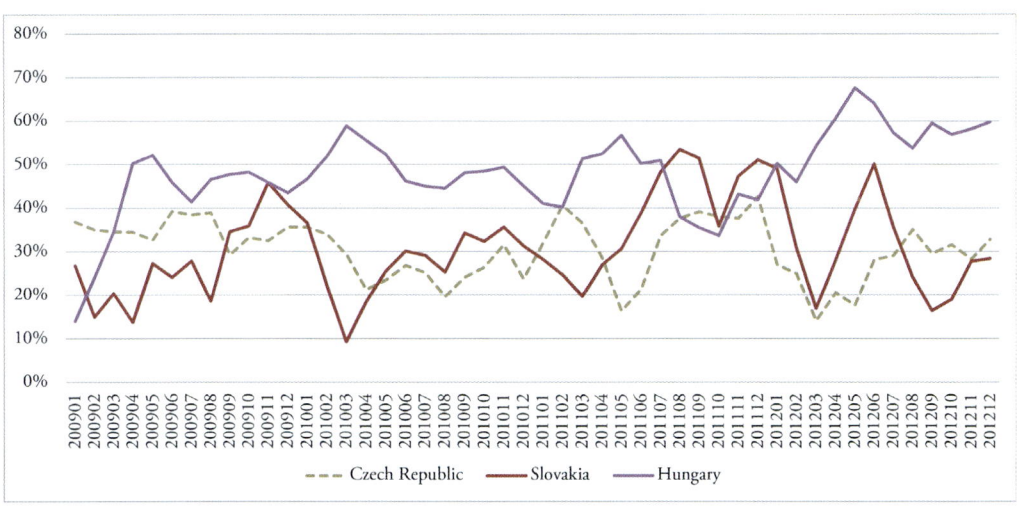

Figure 1. Proportion of contract value making use of EU funding to total contract value, 2009-12, by country (% of total contracted value*, 3-month rolling averages).

Notes: * contract values are converted to EUR using the average exchange rate of the month of contract award, and they are corrected for inflation differentials across the 3 countries. Values are in 2009 Slovak EUR.
Source: PPC

ii. Indicators of institutionalised grand corruption

Developing comparative indicators of institutionalised grand corruption in public procurement for all three countries represents the primary methodological innovation of this article. The approach follows closely the composite indicator building methodology developed by the authors (Fazekas, Tóth and King 2013a) making use of a wide range of public procurement 'red flags'.

The measurement approach exploits the fact that **for institutionalised grand corruption to work, procurement contracts have to be awarded recurrently to companies belonging to the corrupt network**. This can only be achieved, if legally prescribed rules of competition and openness are circumvented. By implication, it is possible to identify the input side of the corruption process, that is techniques used for limiting competition (e.g. leaving too little time for bidders to submit their bids), and also the output side of corruption, that is signs of limited competition: single bid received and recurrent contract award to the same company. By measuring the degree of unfair restriction of competition in public procurement, a proxy indicator of corruption can be obtained. This indicator, called **Corruption Risk Index (CRI) represents the probability of particularistic contract award and delivery in public procurement falling between 0 and 1**. The variables describing the input side of the corruption process in public procurement, that is **elementary corruption techniques**, are reported in **Table 3**.

Table 3. Summary of elementary corruption risk indicators.

Proc. phase	Indicator name	Indicator values	availability CZ	HU	SK
submission	Single bidder contract (valid/received)	1=1 bid received	x	x	x
		0=more than 1 bid received			
	Call for tenders not published in official journal	1=NO call for tender published in official journal	x	x	x
		0=call for tender published in official journal			
	Procedure type	0 =open procedure	x	x	x
		1=invitation/restricted procedure			
		2=negotiation procedure			
		3=other/framework procedures			
		4=outside PP law			
		5=missing/erroneous procedure type			
	Call for tender modification	1=modified call for tenders	x	x	
		0=NOT modified call for tenders			
	Length submission period	Number of days between the publication of call for tenders and the submission deadline (for short submission periods weekends are deducted)	x	x	x

assessment	Number of evaluation criteria	number of distinct evaluation criteria (separate rows)	x	x	
	Length of decision period	number of days between submission deadline and announcing contract award	x	x	x
overall	winner contract share	12-month total contract value of winner / 12-month total awarded contract value (by issuer)	x	x	x
Number of components			8	8	6

Source: PPC.

Component weights are assigned to elementary corruption risk indicators (CRI) using a set of regressions directly modelling corrupt rent extraction in public procurement (**Table 4** and **Table 5**). In these regressions, two likely corrupt outcomes of the corruption process: 1) single bidder contracts and 2) winner's share of issuer's contracts are regressed on elementary corruption risk indicators (**Table 3**) and variables controlling for alternative explanations:
- low administrative capacity: number of employees of the issuer,
- institutional endowments: type of issuer,
- market specificities: CPV division of products procured (2 digit level),
- number of competitors on the market: number of unique winners throughout 2009-12 on CPV level-3 product group (4 digit level) and NUTS-1 geographic region,
- contract size and length, and
- regulatory changes: year of contract award;

and using a restricted sample in order for the regressions to adequately fit a corrupt rent extraction logic as opposed to market specificities or inexperience with public procurement:
- markets with at least 3 unique winners throughout 2009-2012 for markets defined by cpv (level 3) and nuts (level 1) categories for each country; and
- issuers awarding at least 3 contracts in the 12 months period prior to the contract award in question.

For continuous variables such as the length of submission period, **thresholds** had to be identified in order to reflect the non-linear character of corruption. This was done using statistical techniques, in particular analysing the residual distributions.

Regression results indicate that there is considerable market access restriction, hence likely institutionalised grand corruption, going on in all three countries during the 2009-12 period, by and large following the same techniques and 'tricks' (**Table 4** and **Table 5**). These results on their own demonstrate that corruption is systemic in public procurement in these countries. Arriving at robust regression models with considerable explanatory power by using the same regression set-up and variables point at the feasibility of cross-country measurement.

While there is not enough space to discuss each variable in detail, some examples show the logic of analysis and our approach to interpretation. In the **Czech Republic**, the modification of the call for tenders is associated with a 0.6% higher probability of receiving a single bid and with a 1.5% higher winner's contract share. Both results point at a likely interpretation that modifying call for tenders during the bidding phase is systematically used for restricting access and recurrently benefiting the same company. This result warrants that the modification of call for tenders will be part of the Czech CRI. In **Slovakia**, not publishing the call for tenders in the official journal is associated with 9.0% higher probability of a single bidder contract award and a 1.3% higher winner's contract share. Both results suggest that avoiding the transparent and easily accessible publication of a new tender can typically be used for limiting competition to recurrently benefit a particular company. This implies that call for tenders not published in the official journal becomes part of the Slovak CRI. In **Hungary**, leaving only 5 or fewer days, inclusive the weekend, for bidders to submit their bids is associated with 20% higher probability of a single bidder contract and with a 7.9% higher winner's contract share compared to periods longer than 20 calendar days. These indicate that extremely short submission periods are often used for limiting competition and awarding contracts recurrently to the same company. Once again, this provides sufficient grounds for including this category in the Hungarian CRI.

Following this logic, only those variables and variable categories are included in CRI which are in line with rent extraction logic and proven to be significant and powerful predictors in at least one of the two regressions for each country.

Table 4. Binary logistic regression results on contract level, 2009-12, by country, average marginal effects, for markets where nr. of winners >=3.

	Dependent var: single bidder contract (1), multi-bidder contract (0)				
Independent vars-CZ	CZ	Independent vars-SK	SK	Independent vars-HU	HU
NO call for tenders in off. journal	0.116***	NO call for tenders in off. journal	0.091***	NO call for tenders in off. journal	0.098***
Prob.	0.000	Prob.	0.000	Prob.	0.000
procedure type		procedure type		procedure type	
ref. cat.=open procedure		ref. cat.=open procedure		ref. cat.=open procedure	
1=invitation procedure	-0.042***	1=invitation procedure	0.01	1=invitation procedure	0.082***
Prob.	0.000	Prob.	0.575	Prob.	0.000
2=negotiation procedure	0.4***	2=negotiation procedure	0.498***	2=negotiation procedure	0.074***
Prob.	0.000	Prob.	0.000	Prob.	0.000
3=outside PP law	-0.087***	3=other procedure types	0.344***	3=other procedure types	0.276***
Prob.	0.435	Prob.	0.000	Prob.	0.000
4=other/missing/erroneous procedure type	-0.049	4=outside PP law	-0.029	4=missing/error	0.025***
Prob.	1.000	Prob.	0.190	Prob.	0.000
modification of call for tenders	0.006***	modification of call for tenders	n.a.	modification of call for tenders	n.a.
Prob.	0.000				
short submission period		short submission period		short submission period	
ref.cat.=s.period>55*		ref.cat.= s.period>25		ref.cat.=s.period>20	
1= 47<s.period<=55	0.044***	1= 14<s.period<=25	0.078***	1= 17<s.period<=20	0.001
Prob.	0.000	Prob.	0.000	Prob.	0.875
2= 43<s.period<=47	0.067***	2= s.period<=14	0.02	2= 5<s.period<=14	0.103***
Prob.	0.000	Prob.	0.680	Prob.	0.000
3= 38<s.period<=43	0.05***	3= missing	0.064	3= 0<s.period<=5 (incl.weekend)	0.2***
Prob.	0.000	Prob.	0.600	Prob.	0.000
4= 27<s.period<=38	0.007			4=missing	0.05***
Prob.	0.440			Prob.	0.000
5= 0<s.period<=27	0.009				
Prob.	0.230				
6=missing submission period	-0.053				
Prob.	0.455				
number of assessment criteria		number of assessment criteria	n.a.	number of assessment criteria	
ref.cat.= nr.of criteria=0				ref.cat.=2<nr.of criterioa<=4	
1= 0<nr.of criteria<=2	0.053			1=nr.of criterioa=0	0.053***
Prob.	1.000			Prob.	0.000
2= 2<nr.of assessment criteria<=8	-0.006***			2= 0<nr.of criterioa<=2	0.087***
Prob.	0.000			Prob.	0.000
3= 8<nr.of criteria	0.009			4= 4<nr.of criterioa	0.068***
Prob.	0.520			Prob.	0.000
length of decision period		length of decision period		length of decision period	
ref.cat.= 113<dec.period<=201		ref.cat.=62<dec.period<=120		ref.cat.= 44<dec.period<=182	
1= 0<dec.period<=54	0.212	1= 0<dec.period<=62	0.127***	1= 0<dec.period<=32	0.14***
Prob.	0.470	Prob.	0.000	Prob.	0.000
2= 54<dec.period<=67	0.111***	3= 120<dec.period<=227	0.134***	2= 32<dec.period<=44	0.056***
Prob.	0.000	Prob.	0.000	Prob.	0.000
3= 67<dec.period<=100	0.083***	4= 227<dec.period<=322	0.16***	4= 182<dec.period	0.16***
Prob.	0.000	Prob.	0.000	Prob.	0.000
4= 100<dec.period<=113	0.053***	5= 322<dec.period	0.173***	missing	-0.045***
Prob.	0.000	Prob.	0.000	Prob.	0.000
6= 201<dec.period	0.075***	6= missing	0.047		
Prob.	0.000	Prob.	0.550		
7= missing decision period	0.128				
Prob.	1.000				
constant included in each regression					
N	39423		16957		32006
Pseudo-R2	0.295		0.231		0.108

Note: * p<0.05; ** p<0.01; *** p<0.001

*Note: * p<0.05; ** p<0.01; *** p<0.001; clustered standard errors clustered by issuer for P(Fisher), Monte Carlo random permutation simulations for P(permute) (200 permutations) using Stata 12.0.*
Source: PPC.

Table 5. Ordinary least squares regression results on contract level, 2009-12, by country, average marginal effects, for markets where nr. of winners >=3.

		Dependent var: winner's contract share in the last 12 months			
Independent vars-CZ	CZ	Independent vars-SK	SK	Independent vars-HU	HU
single bidder contract	0.032***	single bidder contract	0.021***	single bidder contract	0.02***
Prob.	0.000	Prob.	0.000	Prob.	0.000
NO call for tenders in off. journal	-0.002***	NO call for tenders in off. journal	0.013	NO call for tenders in off. journal	0.021***
Prob.	0.000	Prob.	0.055	Prob.	0.000
procedure type		procedure type		procedure type	
ref. cat.=open procedure		ref. cat.=open procedure		ref. cat.=open procedure	
1=invitation procedure	0.015***	1=invitation procedure	0.099***	1=invitation procedure	-0.037***
Prob.	0.000	Prob.	0.000	Prob.	0.005
2=negotiation procedure	0.01***	2=negotiation procedure	-0.014	2=negotiation procedure	0.011***
Prob.	0.000	Prob.	0.115	Prob.	0.025
3=outside PP law	-0.009***	3=other procedure types	0.054***	3=other procedure types	0.03***
Prob.	0.000	Prob.	0.000	Prob.	0.000
4=other/missing/erroneous procedure type	0.004***	4=outside PP law	-0.003	4=missing/error	-0.005
Prob.	0.000	Prob.	0.820	Prob.	0.275
modification of call for tenders	0.015***	modification of call for tenders	n.a.	modification of call for tenders	n.a.
Prob.	0.000				
short submission period		short submission period		short submission period	
ref.cat.=s.period>55*		ref.cat.= s.period>25		ref.cat.=s.period>20	
1= 47<s.period<=55	-0.009***	1= 14<s.period<=25	0.016	1= 17<s.period<=20	0.014***
Prob.	0.000	Prob.	0.170	Prob.	0.000
2= 43<s.period<=47	0.016***	2= s.period<=14	0.036	2= 5<s.period<=14	0.05***
Prob.	0.000	Prob.	0.210	Prob.	0.000
3= 38<s.period<=43	-0.016***	3= missing	-0.019	3= 0<s.period<=5 (incl.weekend)	0.079***
Prob.	0.000	Prob.	0.845	Prob.	0.000
4= 27<s.period<=38	-0.005			4=missing	-0.01***
Prob.	0.735			Prob.	0.485
5= 0<s.period<=27	-0.005***				
Prob.	0.000				
6=missing submission period	0.155**				
Prob.	0.010				
number of assessment criteria		number of assessment criteria	n.a.	number of assessment criteria	
ref.cat.= nr.of criteria=0				ref.cat.=2<nr.of criterioa<=4	
1= 0<nr.of criteria<=2	-0.01			1=nr.of criterioa=0	-0.01***
Prob.	1.000			Prob.	0.010
2= 2<nr.of assessment criteria<=8	0.014			2= 0<nr.of criterioa<=2	-0.005***
Prob.	0.610			Prob.	0.430
3= 8<nr.of criteria	0.092*			4= 4<nr.of criterioa	0.022*
Prob.	0.040			Prob.	0.000
length of decision period		length of decision period		length of decision period	
ref.cat.= 113<dec.period<=201		ref.cat.=62<dec.period<=120		ref.cat.= 44<dec.period<=182	
1= 0<dec.period<=54	0.006	1= 0<dec.period<=62	0.033***	1= 0<dec.period<=32	0.013
Prob.	0.365	Prob.	0.000	Prob.	1.000
2= 54<dec.period<=67	0.008**	3= 120<dec.period<=227	-0.001	2= 32<dec.period<=44	0.017***
Prob.	0.010	Prob.	0.830	Prob.	0.000
3= 67<dec.period<=100	0.011***	4= 227<dec.period<=322	0.016	4= 182<dec.period	0.047***
Prob.	0.000	Prob.	0.205	Prob.	0.000
4= 100<dec.period<=113	0.03***	5= 322<dec.period	0.014	missing	0.026***
Prob.	0.000	Prob.	0.115	Prob.	0.000
6= 201<dec.period	0.001	6= missing	-0.039		
Prob.	0.270	Prob.	0.370		
7= missing decision period	-0.11				
Prob.	1.000				
constant included in each regression					
N	26830		12847		20658
Pseudo-R2	0.294		0.185		0.234

Note: * p<0.05; ** p<0.01; *** p<0.001; clustered standard errors clustered by issuer for P(Fisher), Monte Carlo random permutation simulations for P(permute) (200 permutations) using Stata 12.0.
Source: PPC.

Once the list of elementary corruption risk indicators is determined with the help of the above regressions, each of the variables and their categories receive a component weight (**Table 6**). As we lack the detailed knowledge of which elementary corruption technique is a necessary or sufficient condition for corruption to occur, we assign equal weight to each variable and the sizes of regression coefficients are only used to determine the weights within variables. For example, if there are four significant categories of a variable, then they would get weights 1, 0.75, 0.5, and 0.25 reflecting category ranking according to coefficient sizes. The component weights are normed so that the observed CRI falls between 0 and 1.

The strength of this composite indicator approach is that the individual components of CRI are vulnerable to changes in regulation, competitive environment, or elite power balance on their own, but taken together they are a more **robust proxy of legal corruption over time**.

In an international comparative perspective, a further strength of CRI is that it **balances national specificities with international comparability**. On the one hand, it provides a comparative indicator in as much as the logic of indicator building and the underlying indicators are the same in each country (of course, as much as data availability permits, further work is in progress). On the other hand, component weights and variable category thresholds (e.g. the definition of accelerated procedure in terms of submission period length differs by country and year) reflect the different national contexts. The same overall scale of country level CRI (i.e. 0-1) lends some meaning to the 'which country is more corrupt' question; nevertheless, the primary purpose of the measurement exercise is to go beyond simplistic understandings of corruption and explore the structure of corruption within each context.

Table 6. Component weights of CRI reflecting variable and category impact on corruption outcomes, normed to have an overall sum of 1.

Czech Republic		Slovakia		Hungary	
variable	weight	variable	weight	variable	weight
single bid	0.16	**single bid**	0.17	**single bid**	0.15
NO call for tenders published in o. journal*	0.16	**NO call for tenders published in o. journal***	0.17	**NO call for tenders published in o. journal***	0.15
Procedure type		**Procedure type**		**Procedure type**	
open	0	open	0	open	0
invitation	0	invitation	0.06	invitation	0.11
negotiation	0.16	negotiation	0.17	negotiation	0.07
outside pp law	0	other/framework	0.11	other	0.15
other/missing/error	0	outside pp law	0	missing/error	0.04
		missing/error	0		
Modification of call for tenders	0.16	**Modification of call for tenders**	n.a.	**Modification of call for tenders**	0
Length of submission period		**Length of submission period**		**Length of submission period*****	
s.period>55**	0	s.period>25	0	s.period>20	0

47<s.period<=55	0.08	14<s.period<=25	0.17	17<s.period<=20	0.04
43<s.period<=47	0.16	s.period<=14	0.08	5<s.period<=14	0.11
38<s.period<=43	0.12	missing	0	0<s.period<=5 (incl. weekend)	0.15
27<s.period<=38	0.04			missing	0.07
0<s.period<=27	0.04				
missing	0				
Number of assessment criteria		**Number of assessment criteria**	n.a.	**Number of assessment criteria**	
nr.of criteria=0	0			nr.of criteria=0	0.05
0<nr.of criteria<=2	0			0<nr.of criteria<=2	0.1
2<nr.of criteria<=8	0			2<nr.of criteria<=4	0
8<nr.of criteria	0.16			4<nr.of criteria	0.15
missing	0			missing	0
Length of decision period		**Length of decision period**		**Length of decision period**	
0<dec.period<=54	0.16	0<dec.period<=62	0.17	0<dec.period<=32	0.1
54<dec.period<=67	0.12	62<dec.period<=120	0	32<dec.period<=44	0.05
67<dec.period<=100	0.08	120<dec.period<=227	0.04	44<dec.period<=182	0
100<dec.period<=113	0.04	227<dec.period<=322	0.08	182<dec.period	0.15
113<dec.period<=201	0	322<dec.period	0.13	missing	0
201<dec.period	0.08	missing	0		
missing	0.12				
Winner contract share	0.16	**Winner contract share**	0.17	**Winner contract share**	0.15

Note: * for procedures with missing call for tenders, component weights are proportionately increased to account for missing information on variables: 1) modification of call for tenders; 2) length of submission period; and 3) length of decision period.
** for invitation procedures: submission period>31
*** exact thresholds deviate from the given numbers depending on the year and procedure type, for full description see (Fazekas, Tóth and King 2013b)

3. Corruption risks and particularistic allocation of EU funding

EU funds can exert influence on institutionalised grand corruption in CEE countries in two principal ways: **first, by providing additional funding for public investment hence increasing the pool of potential rents to extract; second, by changing the motivation structure and constraints of corrupt networks**. Motivations and constraints of corruption are different for EU Structural and Cohesion Funds because monitoring may be more intense and thorough, and because national accountability mechanisms may work in a different way when funding comes from outside. The first approach focuses attention on increased amount of spending, whereas the second on the different motivations for and controls of corruption.

The prevalence of corruption and changes in it are approximated by calculating the expected value of public funds allocated in a particularistic way, where the expected value is calculated by relying on standard expected value theory:

**Expected total value of particularistic resource allocation (EUR) =
probability of corruption (%) * total value spent (EUR)**

where the probability of corruption to occur is measured by CRI. This value captures the amount of resources allocated in a particularistic way which, by no means, equates with the value of corruption rents extracted or cost of corruption. Rather, it implies the overall value of public funds most likely available for rent extraction, while this rent very much depends on the profitability and cost structure of benefiting companies (e.g. even in a very corrupt road construction project, something must be built which costs at least some amount to the contractor). The total social cost of corruption is composed of many components of which corruption rent is only one, and perhaps not even the biggest. Imagine, for example the misallocation of public investment to high corruption rent, but low social return projects such as barely used stadiums, which are expensive to maintain.

3.1. Corruption risks of spending more

Institutionalised grand corruption thrives on public resources, especially on public resources whose allocation can be influenced to benefit a small circle of businessmen and politicians without restraint (Soreide 2002). Hence, by increasing the overall value of public procurement spending, corruption risks and corrupt rent extraction increase, unless they are offset by more stringent controls of corruption. This section estimates the increase in corruption risks due to increased spending only, while holding motivations and controls, that is average corruption risks, constant.

As EU regulation prescribes that EU Structural and Cohesion Funds should represent additional spending rather than substituting national spending (European Council 2006), we assumed 100% additionality, including national co-financing. This means that every Euro of EU funding spent in public procurement is considered to come on top of nationally funded public procurement.

For calculating the expected value of particularistic resource allocation due to additional public spending generated by EU funds (for simplicity: additional particularistic resource allocation), CRI of EU funding has to be held constant at the average CRI of nationally funded public procurement. This is for separating the effect of additional spending from the effect of different motivations for and controls of corruption. Hence, the following formula was used:

Expected value of *additional* particularistic resource allocation $_{EU}$ = probability of corruption $_{national\ average}$ * total value spent $_{EU}$

Using this formula, **the value of particularistic resource allocation due to additional public spending generated by EU funds was between 0.9% and 1.8% of national GDPs in 2009-12 in the three countries (Figure 2)**. Differences between the three countries, by implication, are driven by the different (estimated) amounts of EU funds spent through public procurement.

Figure 2. Estimated value of national and EU funded public procurement disbursed in a particularistic way, by country, % of 2009-12 total GDP.

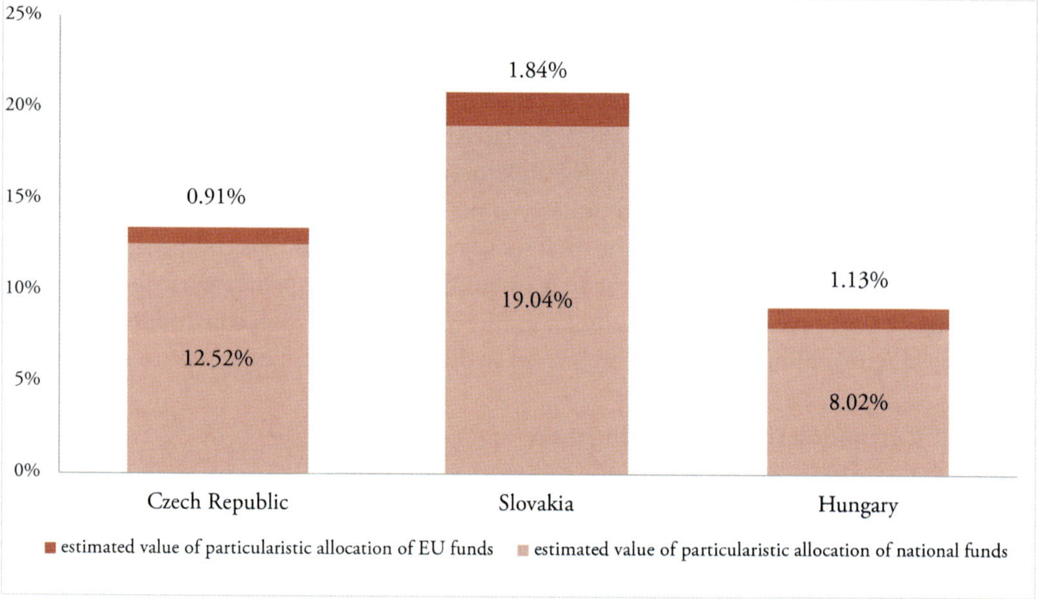

Country	EU funds	National funds
Czech Republic	0.91%	12.52%
Slovakia	1.84%	19.04%
Hungary	1.13%	8.02%

■ estimated value of particularistic allocation of EU funds   ■ estimated value of particularistic allocation of national funds

Source: PPC.

3.2. Corruption risks of spending differently

While additional public resources available for discretionary allocation have considerably increased the prevalence of corruption in the Czech Republic, Hungary, and Slovakia, it is possible that such additional corruption is counterbalanced by more stringent regulation, monitoring, and transparency. If such controls are effective, overall corruption risks would not increase at all or would increase only slightly. In order to check the effectiveness of EU and national institutional frameworks to control corruption of the additional resources, we compare corruption risks (CRI) in public procurement from EU and non-EU funding. Furthermore, the defining aspects of corruption risk differentials are also explored in detail in order to develop policy recommendations.

i. Corruption risks in EU and non-EU funded procurement procedures

In order to identify the causal impact of EU funding on corruption risks, EU and non-EU funded procurement procedures are compared which are as similar in every major respect as possible except for the funding source. As EU funding is not randomly assigned to procurement procedures, we have to rely on state-of-the-art statistical methods to select similar procedures, that is constructing the treatment (EU funding) and control groups (no EU funding). Therefore, first, we show a baseline comparison of CRI between EU and non-EU funded procedures in the three countries; second, we employ propensity score matching.

EU and non-EU funded procurement procedures' CRIs are compared within each country. In Hungary, two alternative comparisons are made: one using a comparative CRI (henceforth hu(comparative)), and another one using a CRI composed of a wider set of indicators (henceforth hu(extended) (for a full description see: Fazekas et al. 2013a). The reason for also including the extended CRI for Hungary is that it paints a richer picture of the driving forces behind the corruption risks of EU funding.

A simple comparison of average CRI scores within each country suggests that EU funded procurement carries higher corruption risks than nationally funded procurement in the Czech Republic and Hungary, while it carries lower corruption risks in Slovakia (Table 7). However, these comparisons may very well be biased as EU and non-EU funded projects could be fundamentally different. For example, if EU funded projects are larger and more complex, then comparisons are inadequate.

Table 7. Naïve comparison of EU and non-EU funded procedures' CRI, 2009-12, by country.

	cz	sk	hu (comparative)	hu (extended)
non-EU funded	0.36	0.522	0.291	0.251
EU funded	0.369	0.421	0.31	0.289
Difference (non-EU - EU funded)	-0.009	0.101	-0.019	-0.038
95% c.interval-lower bound	-0.014	0.092	-0.023	-0.041
95% c.interval-upper bound	-0.005	0.11	-0.015	-0.035
N non-EU funded	26975	14159	25437	25460
N EU-funded	12470	2827	13698	13711

Source: PPC.

The propensity score matching technique employed attempts to select procedures as similar as possible in terms of 1) the main market of procured goods and services; 2) log value of contract; and 3) contract length, as corruption risks can be very different for procurement procedures on different markets and of different sizes or complexities.

Propensity score matching, taking into account confounding factors, reveals a similar picture as above, albeit one different in effect magnitudes (**Figure 3**). The negative effect of EU funding on worsening corruption, has stayed the same in the Czech Republic, while it slightly decreased in Hungary. The positive effect in Slovakia greatly diminished compared to the baseline. All the effects are statistically significant at the 0.001 level. **In the Czech Republic, EU funded projects have 0.011 or 3% higher CRI compared to similar non-EU funded projects. In Slovakia, EU funded projects have 0.065 or 13% lower CRI than similar non-EU funded projects. In Hungary, EU funded projects have 0.01 or 3% higher CRI compared to similar non-EU funded projects using the comparable CRI definition.**

The effect on **Hungarian extended CRI is a great deal larger than for the comparative CRI: 0.022 or 8% higher CRI for EU funded projects than for comparable non-EU funded projects.** This suggests that with corruption risks may come factors associated with the implementation phase such as contract modification (note that Hungary is unique among the three countries in the mandatory publication of every contract modification and contract fulfilment notice). As the differences in driving factors may reveal additional findings, they are explored in the next section.

Figure 3. Average CRI scores of EU and non-EU funded public procurement procedures, by country, 2009-12, $N_{cz}=39320$, $N_{sk}=15760$ $N_{hu}=38862$.

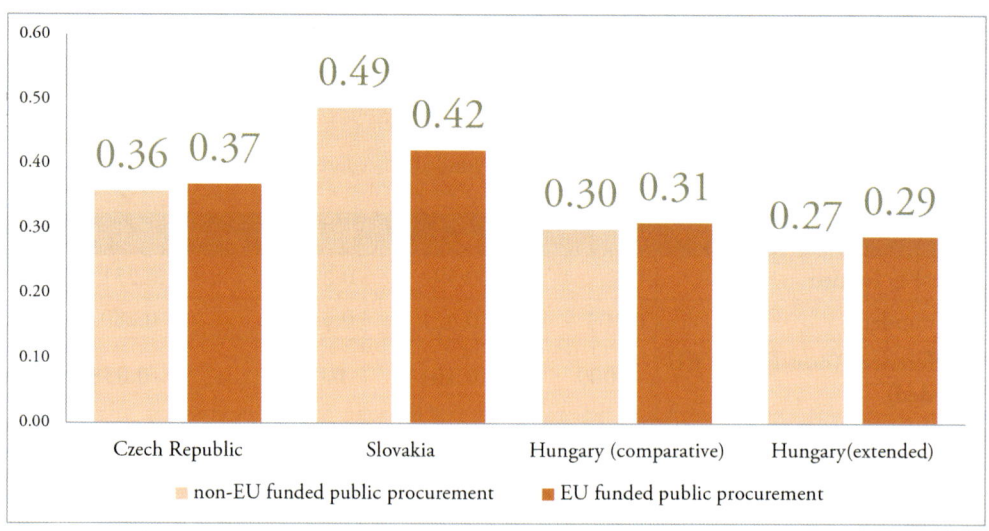

Note: Every within country difference is significant at $p<0.001$ level, standard errors obtained using Monte Carlo random permutations (200 repetitions).

Source: PPC.

In order to get a sense of how big these differences are, we calculated the expected value of particularistic resource allocation due to different motivations and controls of corruption associated with EU Funds (in short expected value of particularistic resources of different source). We used the following formula:

**Expected value of particularistic resources of *different source* $_{EU}$ =
(probability of corruption $_{EU}$ - probability of corruption $_{national\ average}$)
* total value spent $_{EU}$**

Using this formula yields that **in the Czech Republic, the increase in the expected value of particularistic resource allocation due to higher corruption risks of EU funds amounts to 158 million EUR or 0.03% of the total 2009-12 GDP. In Hungary, the same figure is only 52 million EUR or 0.02% of total 2009-12 GDP.** The difference in overall values between the Czech Republic and Hungary are due to lower public procurement spending in Hungary and slightly smaller average effect. **In Slovakia, the expected value of lower average corruption risks associated with EU funds translates into a 381 million EUR or 0.23% of total 2009-12 GDP.** While this positive effect appears very large in comparison to the other two analysed countries, it must be borne in mind that Slovakia seems to have a much higher overall prevalence of institutionalised grand corruption. This improvement of 0.23% of GDP is only a small correction in comparison to the 1.84% of GDP additional particularistic resource allocation (see **Figure 2**). Taken together, the overall effect of EU funds spending in Slovakia is still considerably higher than in the two other countries: 1.61% (1.84% minus 0.23%) as opposed to 0.94% (0.91% plus 0.03%) and 1.15% (1.13% plus 0.02%) for Czech Republic and Hungary, respectively.

Overall, effect sizes are dwarfed by the effect of additional amount of spending, discussed in the previous section. **This implies that the increasing corruption risks due to higher amount of public resources allocated could not be offset by more stringent controls of corruption**. In spite of being designed for controlling fraud and misuse, the EU's monitoring system have failed to moderate increasing corruption risks in Hungary and Czech Republic, while it only partially offset increasing risks in Slovakia. What is most striking is that EU funds are of slightly higher corruption risks in Czech Republic and Hungary than comparable nationally funded procurement procedures calling into question the overall monitoring framework in place in these countries.

ii. Components driving corruption risk differentials

In order to identify the driving factors behind corruption risk differences between EU and non-EU funded public procurement procedures, we performed binary logistic regression with EU funds use on the left-hand side of the equation and corruption risk components on the right-hand side of the equation, while also including the control variables used for propensity score matching.

The comparison of elementary corruption risk indicators driving CRI differences between EU and non-EU funded procurement procedures reveals a remarkably consistent picture across the three countries (**Table 8**). First, EU funded procedures perform better in highly visible formally required aspects of procurement such as publishing the call for tenders, using open procedure type, or allowing sufficient time for bidders to bid. Second, less strictly regulated aspects such as period of time for making an award decision, call for tender modification, or complexity of assessment criteria represent consistently higher corruption risks for EU funded projects. Third, the key dimension according to which **EU funded projects are underperforming is corruption risks associated with lack of competition**: single bidder contract award and winners' contract share. The extensive efforts to make EU funded projects high value for money through competition seem to be insufficient.

Taking into account the broader set of elementary corruption risk indicators in Hungary alters the picture considerably. First, the detrimental corruption risk effect of weak competition remains very strong. Second, the effects of procedure type, submission period length, and decision period length have become insignificant or only weakly negative. Third and most importantly, some less visible procurement corruption risk characteristics take on a crucial role in increasing EU funds corruption risks: weight of non-price evaluation criteria, length of eligibility criteria, and contract modification during delivery.

Table 8. Summary of driving factors of CRI differences between EU and non-EU funded projects, 2009-12.

variable/country	cz	sk	hu(comp)	hu(ext)
Winner contract share	++	++	++	++
Single bid	+	+	+	+
NO call for tenders published in o. journal	- -	-	-	-
Procedure type	- -	-/+	-	0
Length of submission period	- -	- -	- -	-/0
Length of decision period	-/+	-/+	-/0	-/0
Modification of call for tenders	+			0
Number of assessment criteria	-/0		-/+	
Weight of non-price evaluation criteria				++
Length of eligibility criteria				++
Relative price of documentation				-
Annulled procedure re-launched subsequently				-
Contract modification				++
Contract lengthening				- -

Note: - - means strong negative effect on EU funds corruption risks; - means weak negative effect on EU funds corruption risks; + means weak positive effect on EU funds corruption risks; ++ means strong positive effect on EU funds corruption risks; 0 means insignificant or negligible effect on EU funds corruption risks; representing two signs in the same cell indicates a diverse effect of corruption risk categories within the same variable.
Source: own calculation

Conclusions and policy consequences

While much additional work is needed, this paper has already demonstrated that it is feasible and fruitful to use detailed, contract-level data for tracking corruption risks over time across EU countries. Such monitoring can be done in real-time if the necessary investment into database development is made. Fazekas et al. (2013b) discusses data availability in Europe and beyond in detail.

Our preliminary findings indicate that EU funding considerably increase corruption risks in Central and Eastern Europe in at least two principal ways (**Figure 4**). First, by making a large amount of additional public resources available for rent extraction in public procurement; second, by failing to implement sufficient controls of corruption counter-balancing additional resources for corruption. In spite of extensive monitoring efforts of EU authorities, EU funded procurement spending represents even higher corruption risks than the comparable national spending in Czech Republic and Hungary. EU funded public procurement in Slovakia carries only slightly lower corruption risks than comparable national procurement spending, albeit national spending is generally of much higher corruption risk than in the two other countries. In either case, this positive effect falls long way short of offsetting the negative effect of increased discretionary spending available. Nevertheless, the comparatively better performance of Slovakian public procurement projects funded by the EU suggests that EU funding can have a somewhat positive effect in a very high corruption risk environment. Based on this finding further research could look at the conditional effect of EU funding on corruption.

For the three countries combined, our results imply an estimated additional particularistic resource allocation worth up to 1.20% of combined GDP of the three countries throughout 2009-12. This is the result of an estimated maximum 1.23% of GDP in terms of additional funding disbursed in a particularistic way, and an estimated maximum 0.03% of GDP in terms of lower corruption risk of EU funded procurement than national procurement. These figures are exceptionally high, for example compared to total EU funds allocation to these countries, which is about 3.3% of their GDP.

While EU funded public procurement may be effective in lifting growth rates in Central and Eastern Europe, its desired benefits stand in contrast with corruption risks and potential corruption costs. While further work is needed to get more precise estimates of particularistic resource allocation and the associated corruption costs, our preliminary findings already indicate that such costs may not be negligible.

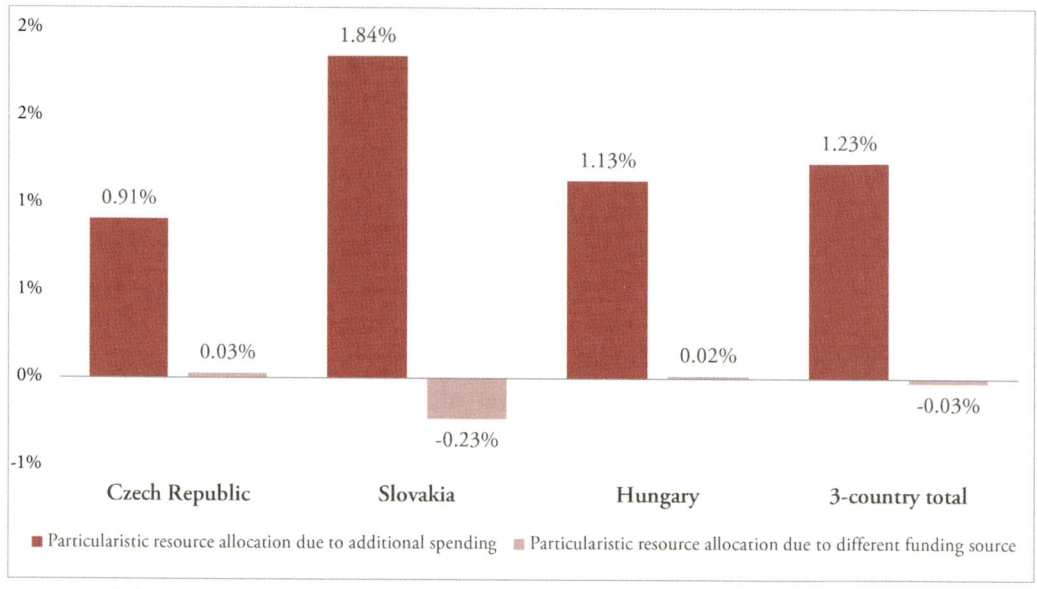

Figure 4. Estimated value of additional particularistic resource allocation due to EU funding in national public procurement, decomposition into effect of additional spending and different funding source, by country, % of 2009-12 total GDP.

Source: PPC

Looking at the driving forces behind corruption risks in EU funding reveals that salient, easily controlled corruption risks are considerably lower, while risks of more subtle procedure characteristics and overall strength of competition considerably increase corruption risks in EU funded public procurement procedures. These findings highlight the importance of monitoring the whole project cycle from initiation to completion as well as the need for a wide indicator set for adequately measure corruption.

If further research confirms the higher corruption risks associated with EU funds, the EU will have to consider implementing more effective policies for protecting its financial interests and promoting good government; in particular:

- **Introducing an EU-wide, real-time monitoring mechanism of EU funds spending designed to detect systematic fraud and corruption in public procurement using data mining techniques, elements of which can be derived from ANTICORRP research;**
- **Refocusing the monitoring and control mechanisms from procedural adequacy to supporting effective competition and controlling bid rigging; and**
- **Considering the reallocation of EU funding going into discretionary investment projects, which typically constitute high corruption risks, towards non-discretionary spending such as unemployment benefit.**

References

Bräutigam, D. A. (2000) *Aid Dependence and Governance*, Stockholm: Almqvist and Wiksell International

Dimulescu, V., Pop, R. and Doroftei, I. M. (2013) 'Corruption risks with EU funds in Romania', *Romanian Journal of Political Science*, 13(1), pp. 101–23

Djankov, S., Montalvo, J. and Reynal-Querol, M. (2008) 'The curse of aid', *Journal of Economic Growth*, 13(3), pp. 169–94

Epstein, R. A. and Sedelmeier, U. (Eds.) (2009) *International influence beyond conditionality: postcommunist Europe after EU enlargement*, London: Routledge

European Commission (2003) *A Comprehensive EU Policy Against Corruption*. Brussels

European Council (2006) *Laying down general provisions on the European Regional Development Fund, the European Social Fund and the Cohesion Fund and repealing Regulation* (EC) No 1260/1999, Pub. L. No. Council Regulation (EC) No 1083/2006, European Union

European Court of Auditors (2012) *Annual Report on the Implementation of the Budget concerning financial year 2011*, Brussels

European Court of Auditors (2013) *Are EU Cohesion Policy funds well spent on roads?* Luxembourg: European Court of Auditors

Fazekas, M. and Tóth, I. J. (2012a) 'Hibák, javításokéselőzeteseredmények - magyarországiközbeszerzések 2010-2011', *Corruption Research Centre*, Budapest

Fazekas, M. and Tóth, I. J. (2012b) 'Public Procurement, Corruption and State Capacity in Hungary – objective measures and new insights', *Corruption Research Centre*, Budapest

Fazekas, M., Tóth, I. J. and King, L. P. (2013a) 'Anatomy of grand corruption: A composite corruption risk index based on objective data', No. CRC-WP/2013:02, *Corruption Research Centre*, Budapest

Fazekas, M., Tóth, I. J. and King, L. P. (2013b) 'Corruption manual for beginners: Inventory of elementary 'corruption techniques' in public procurement using the case of Hungary', No. CRC-WP/2013:01, *Corruption Research Centre*, Budapest

Fazekas, M., Tóth, I. J. and King, L. P. (2013c) 'Hidden Depths. The Case of Hungary'. In A. Mungiu-Pippidi (Ed.), *Controlling Corruption in Europe* vol. 1, Berlin: Barbara Budrich Publishers, pp. 74–82

Goetz, K. H. (2001) 'Making sense of post-communist central administration: modernization, Europeanization or Latinization?' *Journal of European Public Policy*, 8(6), pp. 1032–51

Knack, S. (2001) 'Aid Dependence and the Quality of Governance: Cross-Country Empirical Tests', *Southern Economic Journal*, 68(2), pp. 310–29

KPMG. (2012) EU Funds in Central and Eastern Europe. 2011, Warsaw, Poland: KPMG

Mauro, P. (1998) 'Corruption and the composition of government expenditure', *Journal of Public Economics*, 69, pp. 263–79

Meyer-Sahling, J.-H. (2011) 'The Durability of EU Civil Service Policy in Central and Eastern Europe after Accession', *Governance: An International Journal of Policy, Administration and Institutions*, 24(2), pp. 231-60

Mungiu-Pippidi, A. (2006) 'Corruption: Diagnosis and Treatment', *Journal of Democracy*, 17(3), pp. 86-99

Mungiu-Pippidi, A. (2007) 'EU Accession is no 'End of History'', *Journal of Democracy*, 18(4), pp. 8-16

Mungiu-Pippidi, A. (ed.) (2013) *Controlling Corruption in Europe. The Anticorruption Report 1*, Berlin: Barbara Budrich Publishers

North, D. C., Wallis, J. J. and Weingast, B. R. (2009) *Violence and Social Orders. A Conceptual Framework for Interpreting Recorded Human History*, Cambridge, UK: Cambridge University Press

Rothstein, B. and Teorell, J. (2008) 'What Is Quality of Government? A Theory of Impartial Government Institutions', *Governance*, 21(2), pp. 165–90

Soreide, T. (2002) *Corruption in public procurement Causes, consequences and cures*, Bergen, Norway

Soudek, J. and Skuhrovec, J. (2013) 'Public Procurement of Homogeneous Goods: the Czech Republic Case Study', IES Working Paper 05/2013, IES FSV, *Charles University*, Prague

Tanzi, V. and Davoodi, H. (2001) 'Corruption, growth, and public finances'. In A. K. Jain (Ed.), *The Political Economy of Corruption,* New York: Routledge, pp. 89–110

Transparency International Slovakia (2009) *Open public procurement*. Retrieved October 08, 2013, Available from: <http://tender.sme.sk/en/pages/about>

6. Why Control of Corruption Works - When it Does
ALINA MUNGIU-PIPPIDI[1]

Why do some societies manage to establish control of corruption and others not? Control of corruption is defined here as the capacity of a society to constrain individual corrupt behaviour (defined as particular distribution of public goods leading to undue private profit) in order to enforce the norm of individual integrity in public service and politics as well as to uphold a state that is free from capture by particular interest. This shortened version of the ANTICORRP milestone report explains the causes of the global fight and stagnation against corruption. It uses 2013 data to explain why societies around the world that feel their governments act for their self-interest alone call this corruption. The full version can be read at anticorrp.eu/publications.

Once evidence exists that what is called corruption is a governance context and not an individual behaviour the question on why certain societies have evolved to achieve ethical universalism and control of corruption and others have not becomes the major research question replacing the mis-conceptualized one of 'what causes corruption' (Nield 2002), but retaining the chief question about causality. This report will address that from its interdisciplinary perspective by offering:

1. A theoretical general answer explaining national control of corruption or its opposite, generalized corruption (particularism); in other words, explaining individual behaviour in a given governance context.
2. The statistical tests to support the theory, in other words by explaining what makes some societies more effective than others at controlling corruption.
3. A test of the major policies and institutional interventions used against corruption or with the potential to affect it - always controlling for structural factors.

The means to realize objectives is a large-N comparison method, wherein econometric methods will be used to test factors of interest across as many countries as possible (data allowing). For our dependent variables, we shall use the aggregated Control of Corruption Index (CoC) from the World Bank, the Corruption Risk Index from the International Country Risk Guide (ICRG), experience of bribery from the Global Corruption Barometer 2012, experience of bribery and the perception of favouritism from ANTICORRP's own QOG survey and tolerance towards corrupt practices from World Values Survey 2008. A methodological justification of those choices can be found in our previous 'Trends' report of August 2013 (Mungiu-Pippidi 2013).

---
[1] Roberto Martínez Kukustschka and Ramin Dadasov have contributed analyses for this report.

1. Understanding corruption as a dependent variable

Most anti-corruption strategies are designed to deal with bribery. However, if corruption is considered from a holistic perspective, as we do here, then bribery is just the tip of the iceberg. When answering questions about corruption, survey respondents consider favouritism and offer assessments of their own society's general capacity to enforce public integrity and ethical universalism, rather than considering corruption as it is legally defined in criminal codes. The answers that respondents give to surveys on corruption are filtered by the respondents' general assessment of whether control of corruption works or not in their own country. Two out of three from the 114,000 respondents in 107 countries interviewed for the 2013 Global Corruption Barometer (GCB) consider that favouritism is the rule not the exception in their public service (with only a quarter having resorted to bribes in the year previous to survey) and over 50% believe their governments is captured by vested interests and that corruption has increased, not decreased in the last year.

The argument in favour of control of corruption as the societal capacity preventing institutional corruption (or of particularism as a governance order) is based on the following evidence:

1. **All corruption perceptions reflecting the overall capacity of a society to enforce merit and honesty versus connections or privilege are correlated and a holistic view exists on the country's performance in that respect.** The popular perceptions of corruption take into account all aspects of life (e.g. school, career and public life) and expose the mechanism of advancement in a society and the way the state operates (see **Table 1**). Countries ranked higher for perception of corruption in the Global Corruption Barometer also have higher scores for bribery, the importance of connections for getting things done and show a greater belief that big interests run the government.

2. **Bribery is significantly associated with complex of perceptions (national corruption), but explains very little of it, because bribery is only the result of more complex arrangements that explain differential access to social allocation.** In nearly every survey we find a large gap between corruption victimization (having been asked for a bribe) and perception of corruption (assessment of how many public officials are corrupt), with overblown samples assessing high levels of corruption and low levels of direct experience (see **Figure 1**). Despite this gap, when explaining corruption perception we do find that higher levels of experience of bribery are significantly associated with higher perception of corruption. We simply have to 'top up' exposure to bribery with other experiences and behaviour, to fill the gap. Those factors are captured in **Table 1**.

Table 1. The faces of particularism.

VARIABLES		% of respondents who think that personal contacts are important/very important to get things done in the public sector	% of respondents who think that the government is to 'a large extent' or 'entirely' run by a few big interests	% of respondents that have paid a bribe at least once	% of respondents who consider public officials/civil servants as 'very corrupt' or 'extremely corrupt'	Perception of corruption of public officials/civil servants (weighted average)
% of respondents who think that personal contacts are important/very important to get things done in the public sector	Pearson Correlation	1				
	Sig. (2-tailed)					
	N	104				
% of respondents who think that the government is to 'a large extent' or 'entirely' run by a few big interests	Pearson Correlation	0.647**	1			
	Sig. (2-tailed)	0.000				
	N	98	98			
% of respondents that have paid a bribe at least once	Pearson Correlation	0.145	0.348**	1		
	Sig. (2-tailed)	0.141	0.000			
	N	104	98	105		
% of respondents who consider public officials/civil servants as 'very corrupt' or 'extremely corrupt'	Pearson Correlation	0.471**	0.547**	0.472**	1	
	Sig. (2-tailed)	0.000	,000	0.000		
	N	101	96	101	101	
Perception of corruption of public officials/civil servants (weighted average)	Pearson Correlation	0.505**	0.561**	0.372**	0.970**	1
	Sig. (2-tailed)	0.000	0.000	0.000	0.000	
	N	103	97	104	101	104

** *Correlation is significant at the 0.01 level (2-tailed).*
Source of data: Global Corruption Barometer 2013.

Figure 1. Weight of bribery experience among respondents perceiving high corruption.

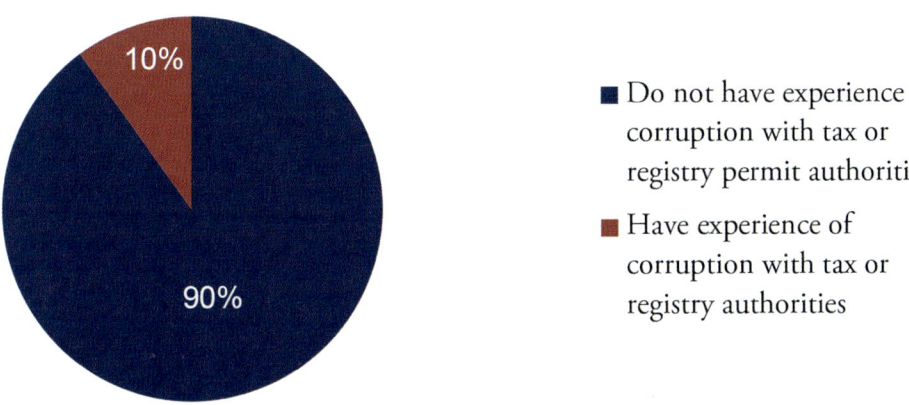

Source of data: Global Corruption Barometer 2013.

3. **Control of corruption (the aggregate) and bribery are explained by different factors, with structural factors being very important in the first case (Treisman 2000) and circumstantial factors very important in the second.** Bribery is not easily determined by wealth or education, for example, but these factors do explain why more or less bribery is to be found in a given country: Any individual might offer a bribe in a context where control of corruption is weak and social determinism is far stronger than the individual. Evidence for the logic of this governance order which shows that where particularism is the rule of the game, bribery develops as a way to counter other types of favouritism (for example, where the individual or company who is not part of some network of privilege has to buy its way in), with favouritism far more widespread than bribery and no correlation between them (see **Table 1**). Furthermore, of the majority of GCB 2013 respondents who thought the public service is very or entirely corrupt, more than two thirds actually were thinking of favouritism, meaning privilege arising out of patronage, nepotism, or connections, when making their assessment (see **Figure 2**). It is therefore favouritism which fills in the gap from point 2.

Figure 2. Weight of connections by respondents perceiving high corruption.

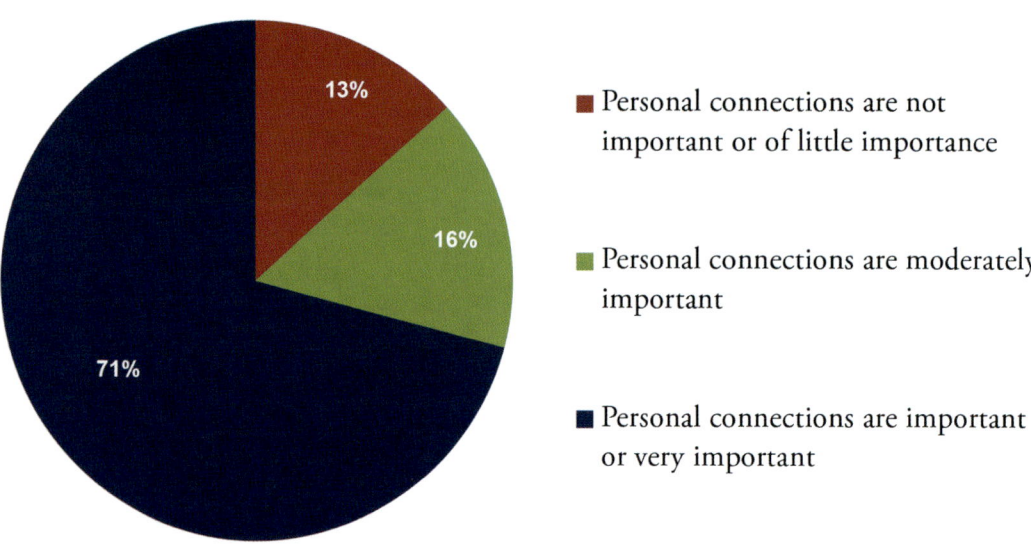

Source: Global Corruption Barometer 2013.

Additionally, and proving that the primary problem is a modus operandi of the state on the basis of particularism we find that satisfaction with public service is inferior for bribers who have to grease the wheels of service compared with the rest of its users across all services who do not need to furnish a supplementary fee to get things done (see **Table 2**).

Table 2. Satisfaction with public service by bribe.

Sector/Service		% of respondents not satisfied with the service	% of respondents satisfied with the service	% of respondents with contact
Education	Paid bribes	32	49	38
	Did not pay bribes	12	66	
Health	Paid bribes	40	42	82
	Did not pay bribes	18	67	
Police	Paid bribes	52	30	22
	Did not pay bribes	16	65	

Source of data: QOG ANTICORRP survey 2013.

In most cases the motivation for bribery is the need among those who are lower on power distance to access a service on an equal footing, because they do not have the necessary connections. When we look at the health sector in the EU and some neighbouring countries, we see that only 36% of the people in the West European core group feel like there are inequalities in the way people are treated. This figure increases to 42% in the group of Mediterranean countries and 47% in accession and aspiring countries (with Turkey doing far better than the Ukraine). The proportion of citizens perceiving unequal treatment in the health care sector then turns into a majority (53% of respondents) in the new EU Member States (**Table 3**). Moreover, the overwhelming majority of people who report having some experience of bribery (between 87% and 98% across regions) come from the group who accuse the health care sector of not treating them equally, and who thus say they have to resort to bribery to ensure access (**Table 3**). Favouritism and bribery therefore fall into place within a larger governance regime placed somewhere on the continuum between particularism and ethical universalism. Finally, again proving the holistic character of corruption, we find that societies which perceive much favouritism and corruption also believe that merit has little to do with social advancement and success in life.

Table 3. Incidence of bribery and perception of equality in health care.

Region	Equal treatment in the public health care system		Unequal treatment in the public health care system	
	% of respondents who agree that everyone is treated equally in the public health care system	% of bribe payers who perceive equal treatment	% of respondents who think they are treated unequally in the public health care system	% of bribe payers who perceive unequal treatment
Northern Europe	64	2	36	98
Mediterranean Europe	58	7	42	93
New EU Members	47	13	53	87
Non- EU Members	53	10	47	90

Source of data: QOG ANTICORRP survey 2013.

Many scholars and policymakers dismiss data extracted from corruption surveys because it is based on 'perceptions'. However, according to the GCB 2013, countries where perception of corruption is high are nevertheless significantly associated with low public expenditure on health (e.g. hospital queues in Brazil), but high on various government projects (from Brazil's expensive World Cup to President Ben Ali's grandiose and empty mega-mosque in Tunis), reduced absorption of assistance funds, low returns from public investment and low participation of women in the labour market and politics (cf. Holmberg et al. 2009). This shows that respondents actually have numerous cues other than their experience with bribery to assess whether or not they are poorly governed.

Leaving aside the complex relationship between corruption and development with its reverse causality problems (corruption may hinder development, but in poor countries which do not pay their policemen or doctors at all or only insufficiently, corruption also funds such services directly), evidence exists of some indisputable consequences of corruption, which again pleads for a holistic approach to control of corruption: High corruption is associated with massive brain drain, as the best educated flee to more meritocratic countries, therefore further subverting their own country's investment in education and finally development itself (Mungiu-Pippidi 2013; Ariu and Squicciarini 2013). That highlights the mechanism by which corruption is so detrimental: Corruption generates high opportunity costs through the subversion of fair competition in diverse sectors, from admission exams into public schools to public sector employment and from a biased allocation of public funds to an unequal treatment of taxpayers'. Perceptions are redeemed by what are extremely close associations with such negative phenomena. Corruption on a national scale thus creates disincentives for merit: in the ANTICORRP QOG 2013 survey of 88,000 Europeans, only citizens in Northern European countries agreed that for the most part advancement in the public or private sector is based on hard work and competence, while for the rest favouritism through connections, the most insidious and widespread form of corruption, seems the ticket to success in their societies (Charron 2013).

Just as individual behaviour has to be placed in a certain governance context, the state too must be understood in the context of a given society. Social allocation reflects the power distance in a society and the dominant exchange mode, based on either performance (market) or rent-seeking (violence, corruption). Particularism is the wider governance regime indicating the dominant norm and behaviour. In a society ruled by particularism, favouritism would be the main social allocation mode, with widespread use of connections of any kind, exchange of favours and, in their absence, monetary inducements. Particularism in a society operates mostly to the advantage of those with more power resources, but no simple elite-theory type explains it. The weaker have their defences, resorting to patronage, cheating, bribery, tax evasion and a variety of other practices to reduce inequality (Scott 1972) once they perceive that the social contract imposed to them is unfair. Elites in societies with a great deal of particularism enjoy a culture of impunity, a culture mirrored by the self-indulgence of the rest of the population who see the behaviour of elites as their best excuse for their own behaviour. By and large, vertical and horizontal exchange networks intersect to create the systemic nature of the problem (Johnston 2005), which remains the particular character of transactions (della Porta and Vanucci 1999).

The most powerful people in such societies would capture the state and channel the distribution of public resources to themselves, their peers and their clients, doing so either openly in neo-patrimonial regimes, or more insidiously in regimes where some competition for power exists, but particularism is the rule. If we cross-tabulate control of corruption measured by the World Bank with the existence of free elections measured by Freedom House (**Table 4**), we can see the distribution of three different governance regimes: Universalism, a regime characterized by a high level of control of corruption is present in the 35 electoral democracies in the upper tercile of control of corruption and in only three non-democratic regimes: Qatar, the United Arab Emirates and Singapore. Although the average score of all democracies, corrupt or non-corrupt, is far better than that of non-democracies (5.33 versus 3.06), the number of neo-patrimonial regimes, defined as corrupt or very corrupt non-democratic polities, is almost the same as the number of corrupt or very corrupt democratic countries i.e. competitive particularistic regimes. As shown in **Table 4**, there are 75 (51 + 24) neo-patrimonial countries versus 79 (22 + 57) competitive particularistic regimes.

Across the three groups we find, as expected, that the countries which are in the upper tercile of control of corruption (the 'universalism' countries) differ significantly from those where particularism is the norm, having almost no bribery, a lower perception of the importance of connections for success and significantly fewer people who believe that a few big interests run the government. Ethical universalism seems then to be more of an ideal benchmark than a real governance regime as only the Scandinavian countries, Australia, New Zealand, Switzerland, the Netherlands and Luxembourg have reached a control of corruption score above 9 (in a recoded scale from 1 to 10 where Denmark ranks as the top performer). The remaining countries in this group range down to a control of corruption score of 6.7. 22 more countries ranging from the Czech Republic to Israel, constitute a 'borderline' group, where the two norms, particularism and universalism, seem to be competing.

Table 4. Governance regimes at a glance.

2012	CoC lowest tercile	CoC mid tercile	CoC top tercile	Total	Average CoC score
Non democratic	51	24	3	78	3.06
Electoral democracies	22	57	35	114	5.33
Total	73	81	38	192	

Source: Control of corruption (World Bank Institute, 2012) recoded 1 to 10 with 10 the best, by electoral democracy as classified by Freedom House.

The top group of democratic achievers looks remarkably compact, old European cultures and some of their colonies, those populated for the majority with people of European descent. Japan alone is different, and is universally acknowledged as the most successful Western-type modernization; and different too are the nondemocratic achievers of good governance. The fact remains that very few original streams remain to explain this group of top achievers, with the Scandinavians, Anglo-Saxons, Central Europeans (Dutch and German) at the top, and the French and the Spanish one step lower in accomplishment. Good governance origins seem therefore to have time and culture boundaries (Neild 2002).

2. Institutional monocropping and the prescription mechanism

While always assisting in some general modernization policies at the state level (e.g., civil service merit-based recruitment, administrative reforms, and support for central audit agency), the international anti-corruption community has concentrated its efforts in the past years on promoting a specific international legislation against corruption and has promoted a few anti-corruption tools for domestic implementation. Over a span of less than fifteen years, policy and legal instruments were identified, agreed upon, and adopted en masse by countries. Donors, consultants, and NGOs set out to implement the control of corruption agenda by selling a limited number of anti-corruption instruments across the globe and by shaping the programs and budgets of development agencies accordingly. Peter Evans (2004, p. 30) described it as: "'institutional monocropping': the imposition of blueprints based on idealized versions of Anglo-American institutions, the applicability of which is presumed to transcend national circumstances and cultures.' It might seem patronizing today that western countries could expect to export their institutions to the rest of the world in the same way that technologies are transferred. However, it bears recalling that this approach broadly worked in countries like Japan, which embarked on its modernization path with a program similar to that of the West, determined in fact to beat the West at its own game. There was likewise a resurgence after 1990 of the belief – differently formulated than in earlier generations – that the 'right' institutions can deliver development and that in their absence external aid does not work. That approach to institutional export is differently motivated, labelled, and marketed than was the case under colonialism, but its central belief – that societies can be modernized by outside intervention through institutional transplants to resemble the West more closely – remains in the end basically unchanged.

The contemporary approach seems no longer driven by imperialism, but by convenience. Many donors are governments, so it is natural for them to advocate their own type of organization to the governments they assist or trade with in the hope that their assistance will generate better returns. Furthermore, good governance strategies based on knowledge transfers to other governments create a labour market for consultants from developed economies and can be easily packed into short-term programs. Anti-corruption strategies anchored in domestic political dynamics are more politically sensitive, labour-intensive and long-term, and therefore far less profitable for external consultants. An anti-corruption industry quickly developed around the international anti-corruption package and began to attract considerable funds and lobbying for more training and capacity-building. But did the anti-corruption industry deliver a panacea?

In his now classic book, Comparative Constitutional Engineering, Giovanni Sartori (1994) warned about the dangers of believing that formal institutions shape countries, showing that long Latin American constitutions had not translated after many decades into anything comparable to democracy as known in the United States, which had been their primary source of inspiration. Douglass North too was aware of local specificities, warning that 'different institutional structures will yield different results' (North in Andrews 2008, p. 381). Furthermore, by copying the formal institutions of present-day Sweden or Denmark, 'one-best-way' transfer models presume that the actual path those countries took to get where they are does not matter. As one critic put it: 'The good governance picture of effective government is not only of limited use in development policy […] It imposes an inappropriate model of government that 'kicks away the ladder' that today's effective governments climbed to reach their current states' (Andrews 2008: 402).

A few examples might help us understand this 'monocropping' better. The Council of Europe's Group of States against Corruption (GRECO), a rotating peer-review system, assesses individual European countries' anti-corruption legislation and recommends that components of a universal repertoire of anti-corruption measures are adopted everywhere, regardless of local circumstances. In 2004, it was the turn of Denmark, which is generally considered to have one of the best-quality governments in the world. GRECO (2009, p. 12) found Denmark's legislation imperfect on the grounds that it was a century old and was not used often enough for prosecutions (because, in fact, it had an effective deterrent effect on corruption). Likewise, in Spring 2012, the Australian government made the news for its refusal to implement UNCAC and adopt a single anti-corruption agency as recommended by UN experts and a parliamentary committee, although the committee then stated that: 'there is very little evidence of serious or systemic corruption in the Australian public service' (Baker and McKenzie 2012). Australia's state anti-corruption agencies (notably New South Wales) had been in the historical vanguard of successful control of corruption and the refusal of the Australian national government to change a system that worked well was perfectly justified - but it was badly received by the global trend of monocropping.

A reputable US-based NGO called Global Integrity created an index which placed countries on a scale reflecting their institutional tools for fighting corruption. In 2011, they abandoned the index with little public explanation. The countries which featured in the top five of the index in the previous two years were in fact extremely corrupt countries which had simply adopted more anti-corruption instruments than anyone else – notably Bulgaria, Romania, and Macedonia, because they were motivated by the need to show progress in their EU accession negotiations (Global Integrity 2011).

Lambsdorff (2008) regressed the two measures of the Global Integrity Index, the legal framework and the actual practice, on TI Corruption Perceptions Index and the 2007 Global Competitiveness Survey of the World Economic Forum (WEF) and found that too many laws can actually hinder control of corruption. What is important is whether or not the laws are practiced. Global Integrity created a good indicator called 'implementation gap' from the difference between legal arrangements and practice, which in the cases of most institutionally 'advanced' countries (where international community's conditionality is stronger, like in the Balkans) can be higher than 50%, showing a major divergence between the 'legal' country and the 'real' country.

Assessments of the impact of this anti-corruption repertoire on corruption levels around the world have not been very systematic. To fill this gap, we focus on five distinct institutional efforts: the ratification of UNCAC, the endorsement of freedom of information legislation/acts (FOIA), the establishment of an anti-corruption agency (ACA), the creation of an office of ombudsman and 'constitutional' interventions. While UNCAC is a recent treaty (2005), the other interventions have been around much longer – as such, their effect, or lack of it, has had more time to materialize. All of those tools have been promoted intensely by the international community, resulting in their importation by a large number of countries (see **Table 5**). FOIA and ACA have been adopted on a massive scale since 2000; an ombudsman was more popular as an accountability tool between 1990 and 2000, following democratic revolutions. The final result, however, is a virtual explosion of institutional imports all around the world.

Table 5. The development of Institutional Interventions.

Year	UNCAC ratifications	Countries with FOIA	Countries with ACA	Countries with ombudsman
1990		15	12	47
2000		42 (27 new)	41 (29 new)	100 (53 new)
2008	145*	86 (44 new)**	98 (57 new)	135 (35 new)

Note: *2003 to 2011 data / **2010 data.
Source: Hertie School of Governance Database[2].

To test the impact of this institutional equipment, two sets of measures were created: one a simple dichotomy indicating the existence of an anti-corruption tool (e.g., an

---

[2] This database was compiled by the Hertie School of Governance for NORAD in 2011 and updated for ANTICORRP in 2013. In the case of UNCAC, the dataset from the website of the United Nations Office on Drugs and Crime, which records information about the ratification of the Convention (applied to 193 countries in our database), was used; in the case of FOIA, Roger Vleugels' (2008) records of the existence of FOIA in countries worldwide were used (applied to 193 countries in our database). In the case of anti-corruption agencies, according to the OECD categorization, 176 countries were checked for the existence, year of establishment and type of anti-corruption agency in 2008. Similarly, a set of 193 countries has been checked for the presence and year of establishment of a working office of the Ombudsman in 2008. The Hertie School datasets record the sole existence (year of establishment and type of an agency in the case of ACA) and do not include any estimate on the efficiency or independence of the institutions.

anti-corruption agency), and another indicating the number of years the tool has been in operation. We documented the adoption of an intervention until 2008, and tested its impact on the 2008, 2010 and 2012 corruption ratings. Two different tests were undertaken: (i) a simpler, descriptive procedure comparing the evolution of corruption over time, before a given intervention (marked as year 0), and submitting it to a significance test; and (ii) bivariate and multivariate regressions for each of the interventions, with controls for development. The ICRG corruption risk was used as the dependent variable for both trend and regression analysis due to its longer time series. It also fits the aim of holistically analysing corruption because, despite its commercial purpose, it attempts to measure particularism rather than just bribery (PRS 2013). However all regressions were also run on CoC (see **Table 6**).

Table 6. Impact of interventions on control of corruption.

VARIABLES	ICRG Risk of Corruption (2010)			WGI Control of Corruption (2012)		
	Model I	Model II	Model III	Model IV	Model V	Model VI
Presence of FOIA	0.65***			1.17***		
	(0.186)			(0.321)		
Presence of ACA		-0.17			-0.39	
		(0.198)			(0.326)	
Presence of Ombudsman			0.15			0.30
			(0.218)			(0.362)
Constant	2.33***	2.77***	2.57***	3.89***	4.61***	4.22***
	(0.136)	(0.155)	(0.186)	(0.217)	(0.235)	(0.304)
Observations	137	138	137	186	191	186
R-squared	0.08	0.01	0.00	0.07	0.01	0.00

Robust standard errors in parentheses / *** $p<0.01$, ** $p<0.05$, * $p<0.10$

The bivariate regressions returned only the presence of a Freedom of Information Act (FOIA) as significant. For the rest, there seems to be no significant difference in the performance of countries which installed an ombudsman or an anti-corruption agency and those which did not. For the before and after significance test two different samples were used, one with all the countries, the other without countries in the top tercile of control of corruption, to allow for more sensitivity to countries which need more change. But in neither circumstance did the control of corruption scores at the end vary significantly compared with the start of intervention, although again the presence of an FOIA is the exception. Otherwise, however, the results of tests support each another showing no significant impact across countries when comparing countries which adopted the intervention with countries which did not. Two different explanations seem to be needed. One question is why do favourite interventions seem to work so poorly? The second is about FOIA: when and in what circumstances does adopting it work?

The UNCAC includes provisions for preventive measures (Chapter II) as well as criminalization and law enforcement (Chapter III). The adoption of an effective follow-up monitoring mechanism for the implementation of the UNCAC is considered to be one of the biggest challenges ahead. Few developing countries have transposed the provisions of the UNCAC into national law, to say nothing of the challenges of implementing them in practice. Considering the reputational costs (international and domestic) for a country that does not adopt the UNCAC, it is to be expected that far more countries must have adopted the treaty than actually meant to implement it. Once every country has adopted the UNCAC - a moment fast approaching - variation will disappear and it will not be worth testing the impact of UNCAC through regression analysis, because too little diversification in the dummy variable will remain. However, the before and after test too shows no significant improvement (**Figure 3**).

Figure 3. ICRG risk of corruption before and after UNCAC ratification.

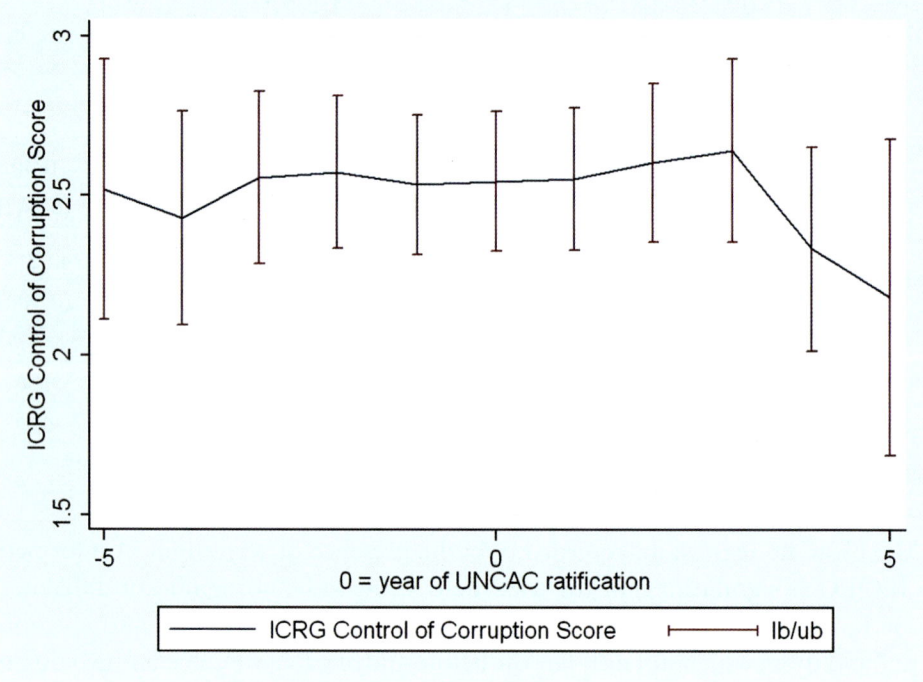

Legend: Evolution of corruption (horizontal line) after ratification of the UNCAC (year zero), when averaged (confidence interval indicated by vertical bar), is non-significant. ICRG corruption scale has the highest number of points indicating the lowest potential risk for that component and the lowest number (0) indicating the highest potential risk. Reference year 2009.
Source: ICRG and Hertie School of Governance database.

The establishment of a dedicated anti-corruption body has been one of the main institutional recommendations in anti-corruption conventions to date. The international community became the major proponent of ACAs, persistently recommending their creation as an important piece of a country's institutional architecture and its large-scale anti-corruption strategies. The forerunners of today's anti-corruption agencies date back to the 1980s and 1990s (e.g., Hong Kong, Singapore, and Australia), when internal corruption scandals and poor performance by conventional law enforcement bodies (e.g., police, courts, and offices of the attorney general) strengthened the position of ACAs as the 'ultimate institutional response to corruption' (de Sousa 2009, p. 2). ACAs were promoted by several conventions on the control of corruption - UNCAC, the African Union Convention, the Inter-American Convention, the Convention of the Council of Europe - as well as by the EU during its enlargement process. But in line with the theory of change presented later in this chapter, we should presume that an anti-corruption agency works only if the rule of law already exists in a given country - otherwise the agency will be either inefficient or used against political opponents by those in power. The main difficulty however is to build rule of law, in other words to convince those in government that they should stand before the law on an equal footing with everyone else. Unsurprisingly, no significant improvement in the corruption risk estimate is found for countries which have adopted the agency compared to the rest. All types of agencies were tested separately, as well as according to OECD categories, with no significant results - a finding in line with earlier reports by Kaufmann (1998) and Meagher (2005). An earlier report has already acknowledged that, in fact, context is the essential element for the success of an agency (Doig et al. 2005). Reports have now started to warn that ACAs can be effective tools only when they respond to a national consensus and are supported by a broad domestic coalition (Heilbrunn 2004, p. 2) and they should not be created without a 'systematic assessment of the local (political) context', for there is a risk that they could use their special powers to engage in a witch-hunt against political opponents, rather than genuinely pursue anti-corruption goals (USAID 2006, p. 5).

But the 'failure' of many agencies is more systemic and stems from the fact that such agencies are simple forms of pleasing donors and as such were created without any intention of enforcement. This is the reported 'prescription mechanism', which operates frequently in relations between the international donor community and a country, e.g. the European Union and candidate countries, when good marks are given to candidates who adopt all suggestions of the donor for reform, without any check on their real implementation, impact or, indeed, the adequacy of the reforms (Mungiu-Pippidi 2007). Similarly, van Aaken et al. (2008) investigated the impact of prosecutorial independence on containing corruption and found that 'de facto' independence decreases corruption, but 'de jure' (formal) independence has little impact.

While the UNCAC does not mention the ombudsman's office in the repertoire of anti-corruption measures, this accountability tool is promoted by donors and by Transparency International as a measure to control corruption. The role of the ombudsman has mostly been related to making administrative law simpler for 'aggrieved persons' wishing to challenge government actions in courts (Brown and Head 2004, p.

5). However, the ombudsman's mandate of protecting citizens from abuse directly addresses favouritism and lack of transparency. Even though nowadays 'the mandate of the ombudsman generally goes beyond corruption cases and includes instances of maladministration attributable to incompetence, bias, error or indifference that are not necessarily corrupt' (UNDP 2005, p. 14), cases exist where the ombudsman is given a mandate to investigate corruption complaints directly and takes on the role of an ACA (e.g., Philippines and Papua New Guinea). In any case, as guarantor of an accountable, impartial, and fair government, the ombudsman as an institution should contribute to better governance through improvement of government accountability (Mungiu-Pippidi et al. 2011). The problem, however, is the same as with ACAs: many such institutions are de facto subordinated to government or parliamentary majority. Historically, the Swedish ombudsman, is strong because it is an instrument of the opposition.

Freedom of Information Acts (FOIAs) have existed longer than UNCAC and ACAs, yet empirical results on their impact have been mixed. Bac (2001, p. 88) argues that greater transparency leads to improved information about whom to bribe, while at the opposite end of the spectrum Islam (2006, p. 153) finds that countries with greater transparency, measured through the existence of FOIA, do have lower corruption rates. By the end of 2003, 46 countries had implemented some form of FOIA (Escaleras et al. 2010, p. 436); by 2008 that number had increased to 82 (Vleugels 2008). The FOIAs differ in strength and measurements exist on how strong or weak a FOIA is; however, all information acts around the world include a few common elements to whit the right to file a claim for information, due process which must be followed (including time frames), legislation which should be enforced, whether a means for appeal exists, whether certain information can be withheld, and if so, by whom (Escaleras et al. 2010, p. 436).

These days, a growing body of treaties, agreements, action plans and other statements urge or require nations to adopt an FOIA. The FOIA clauses are included not only in anti-corruption treaties but also in agreements on environmental protection and natural resources management, as well as in a number of international human rights treaties and regional conventions (Banisar 2006, p. 8). The UNCAC also recommends a variety of measures aimed at improving transparency as a means to fight corruption (Article 10 on 'Public Reporting' and Article 13 on 'Participation of Society'). Additionally, the Universal Declaration on Human Rights and the International Covenant on Civil and Political Rights both require that every person shall have the right to free expression and to seek and impart information (Article 19, the Universal Declaration of Human Rights). Among recently written constitutions from countries in transition (Central and Eastern Europe as well as Latin America) most include a provision on access to information (Mungiu-Pippidi et al. 2011). Additionally, a number of countries with older constitutions (e.g., Finland, Norway) have recently begun amending their constitutions to include right of access to information (Banisar 2006, p. 17).

Figure 4. Improvement in control of corruption after introduction of FOIA.

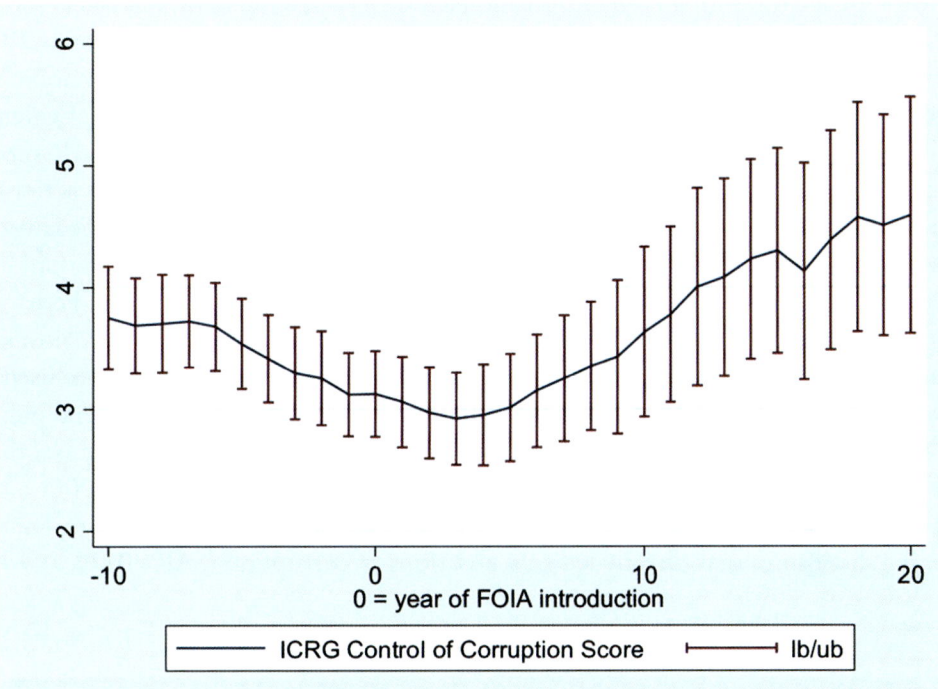

Legend: Evolution of corruption (horizontal line) after introduction of FOIA (year zero), is significant when averaged (confidence interval indicated by vertical bar). ICRG corruption scale from 0 to 6 has the highest number of points indicating the lowest potential risk for that component and the lowest number (0) indicating the highest potential risk.
Source: ICRG and Hertie School of Governance database.

The before and after test results are shown in **Figure 4**, which traces the development of control of corruption from ten years before the implementation of a FOIA (t=-1 to t=-10) to twenty years after its implementation (t=1 to t=20)[3]. The graph shows that there is a downward trend in control of corruption before the implementation of an FOIA, followed by an upward trend, which starts a few years after its implementation. To establish whether the corruption score changed significantly after the implementation of an FOIA, t-tests were run, comparing the mean corruption score at t=0 with the means from later years, up to twenty years following the introduction of an FOIA. Taking into consideration the actual t-test, the increase in corruption score becomes significant at the 5% level two years after the implementation of a FOIA and remains so for twenty years after its introduction. FOIA is also the only intervention significant in bivariate regressions on control of corruption. But how robust is this finding? Although it is a significant determinant of control of corruption in bivariate regressions, the impact is weakened when controlled for development as shown by the results in

---

[3] The graphs were produced using the xtgraph procedure in STATA, showing averages of a single outcome measured at several points over time. Standard errors and confidence intervals are calculated separately for every time point, using the t-distribution. See also Mungiu-Pippidi et al. 2011 for more details.

Table 7. Transparency remains positively associated with control of corruption, if we control for the rural-urban dimension and civil society development, but is less robust when life expectancy is introduced as a control (significant on CoC, but not on ICRG's Risk of Corruption). Its impact seems to be stronger at mid to high levels of development and to be due to non-state actors playing a large role in its implementation. Evidence collected by Transparency International, the Open Society Institute, and SAR shows that a successful FOIA goes hand in hand with civil society and citizen activism. Implementation was poor (Kocaoglu and Figari 2006) in countries where the law was adopted as part of a top-down government reform plan (e.g., Albania), as an international initiative (e.g., Bosnia) or as a result of lobbying from civil society elite (e.g., Peru). By contrast, in counties where civil society coalitions pressed for access laws (e.g., Slovakia, Romania and Bulgaria), the resulting legislation, even if far from perfect, was used as a weapon for disclosure by civil society, journalists, and members of the general public alike. Monitoring in Bulgaria and Romania already showed that by 2006 more than 50% of requests filed elicited the information sought (Kocaoglu and Figari 2006) and that NGOs were winning spectacular litigation cases against government in courts, forcing disclosures that directly led to accusations of corruption (SAR 2011).

Table 7. Impact of freedom of information on control of corruption.

VARIABLES	ICRG Risk of Corruption (2010)		WGI Control of Corruption (2012)	
	Model I	Model II	Model III	Model IV
Presence of FOIA	0.31*	0.59***	0.23	0.92***
	(0.167)	(0.165)	(0.304)	(0.300)
CSOs per capita	0.02***	0.02***	0.01**	0.02**
	(0.006)	(0.006)	(0.006)	(0.006)
Life expectancy	0.06***		0.14***	
	(0.009)		(0.015)	
Rural Population		-0.02***		-0.05***
		(0.004)		(0.007)
Constant	-2.10***	2.98***	-5.88***	5.82***
	(0.603)	(0.223)	(1.015)	(0.394)
Observations	131	130	163	162
Adj. R-squared	0.37	0.32	0.41	0.34

Note: Robust standard errors in parentheses / *** $p<0.01$, ** $p<0.05$, * $p<0.10$

The hypothesis that the interaction between transparency and activism from civil society together exert an effect was confirmed in our analysis: The introduction of an interaction between the number of civil society organizations and a fiscal transparency measurement, Open Budget Index (OBI), makes the Civil Society Organization per capita variable lose its significance which exists in the bivariate equation, while both FOIA and the interaction remain significant (**Table 8**). Practically, that means that the disclosure of public budgets would have a positive effect on control of corruption, provided always that civil society is strong and able to participate successfully as an actor in budgetary oversight. The fact that FOIA remain highly significant with all these controls also confirms that among all interventions they have the greatest potential - provided some sort of civil society exists or is under development.

Table 8. FOIA and interaction between fiscal transparency and civil society.

VARIABLES	ICRG Risk of Corruption	
	Model I	Model II
HDI	26.97***	25.80***
	(7.352)	(7.526)
ICT	0.112	0.117
	(0.103)	(0.105)
FOIA presence	0.0754***	0.0744***
	(0.0167)	(0.0161)
Political stability	3.976***	3.988***
	(1.076)	(1.076)
Open Budget Index (OBI)	0.00823	0.0314
	(0.0492)	(0.0602)
Number of CSOs	0.0177***	0.00588
	(0.00523)	(0.0142)
Interaction OBI*CSO		0.000180*
		(0.000204)
Constant	-13.82**	-11.68*
	(5.900)	(6.364)
Observations	78	78
R-squared	0.542	0.545

Note: Robust standard errors in parentheses / *** $p<0.01$, ** $p<0.05$, * $p<0.10$

Finally, great hope among good governance consultants is invested in reform of political institutions. The rationale for it, however, is unclear. In Italy, for instance, domestic agency has pushed for reforms of the electoral system several times in reference to corruption, but that did not prevent backsliding on CoC from 1996 (first year of measurement) to the present. The mechanism of such persistence in reforming institutions that change nothing seems rather to be related to the external perception of such reforms. Passing a law or even amending a Constitution is simple and can be reported instantly as a successful reform, even if no real control of corruption follows. Persson and Tabellini (2004) have tested a good number of constitutional tools in a sample of 90 countries, finding only one robust effect, the magnitude of electoral districts (i.e. small districts are associated with more corruption), eventually combined with single seat constituencies, which they explain as a measure of open or closed entry into politics. Small districts are actually far easier to gain by patronage and clientelistic allocations, so they favour corruption, in comparison with larger ones, which might require a more programmatic approach to electoral campaigning. In our larger dataset, we were unable to find any significant relationship between electoral systems and control of corruption, testing proportional versus majority systems, closed lists versus the rest, and electoral threshold. Reported results are mixed and controversial in the area of political reforms - particularly concerning federalism (e.g. Treisman 2000 found it associated with corruption), decentralization and electoral systems (Kunicova and Rose-Ackerman 2005; Brown et al. 2005; Chang and Golden 2004; Lederman et al. 2005; Park 2003). Generally, each of these papers covers only a limited number of countries and electoral situations, so the universality and robustness of their findings is uncertain. Another constitutional device without statistical evidence of impact on control of corruption is the establishment of Constitutional Courts.

In the conclusions of this review of the impact of favourite anti-corruption interventions, whether tested alone or with development controls, we suggest that a country does not progress simply because it imports one or other institutional tool - or, indeed, all of them - when state and society actually operate largely by particularism. Our results do not mean that outliers do not exist, nor that such tools are ineffective everywhere and in every context, but they do warn strongly against over-reliance on the institutional toolkit. It may be that an institution such as the ombudsman might have more impact if reformed along the lines of a FOIA - that is, entrusting it to the losers in corrupt arrangements, making them the key stakeholders in the institution rather than subordinating it to Parliaments or Governments, with the attendant risk of their being just as likely to be part of the problem. What is ultimately needed is not a silver bullet, because none exists, but a better alignment of tools with contexts, in particular with already existing human agency in favour of change. Few institutional weapons seem effective, and they will not work on their own, for they need active agents to put them to use in order to achieve success.

3. Critical mass or critical mess? In search of the optimal equilibrium

Despite an exponential increase in work on corruption over the last twenty years, the field remains divided between micro-theoretical models and macro-empirical models at the country level, with much confusion and no real communication between individual, organization and national level. Not only is the disconnect between these levels of analysis a serious impediment, but so too is the absence of time series data which would allow a theory of governance change to develop. There has simply not been enough change in the data since 1984 when the PRS Group started measuring corruption risk to allow valid inference, and older expert scores are even less reliable (PRS also had a change of methodology which makes their time series corruption risk measure to some extent debatable). But change occurred in the twentieth century. Some first generation achievers of good governance continued to evolve during this interval, with the Americans and the British cleansing urban politics of corruption, the French gradually de-politicizing administration, certain British colonies like Australia and New Zealand laying the foundations of an accountable independent government; and so forth. All those developments cannot be captured except by qualitative methods, as we have no quantifiable dependent variable.

Samuel Huntington had already asked the insightful research question in 1968 when he wondered why the modernization process increases, not decreases corruption. Indeed, if modernity is the quintessence of good governance with the build-up of a critical mass of enlightened citizens, accountable politicians and trustworthy magistrates, why does the process of 'getting there' itself look like such a critical mess? Huntington suggested that the answer lies in the transition process between the old social order and new norms, with disputed access to resources for new groups never fully consented to by old elites, leading to the development of informal strategies of social mobility. Many developing and transitional countries have set up a superstructure of rational-legal administration, but particularism continues to be the rule. Modern impersonality and objectivity, which lie at the basis of behaviour in the public domain, including market transactions, do not necessarily emerge in every case, which is why control of corruption has come to be seen by economists like Acemoglu and Robinson (2012) as the major problem of development.

Modernization, as Huntington saw, does not bring about only increased constraints on the behaviour of rulers with the political modernization process (reducing power distance in societies, excepting 20th century totalitarian systems) but with serous growth of public resources (i.e. potential spoils) brings about an increased role for the state to fulfil all the new functions. Historically the two processes seem to have developed in opposite directions (Mungiu-Pippidi 2014). As political discretion decreases and people become citizens in the modern sense, endowed with civil and political rights, potential spoils grow in time due to the state's scope growing, at least until the neo-liberal austerity policies of the late twentieth century, as people begin to pay more and more taxes than before to finance a state which takes more and more tasks upon itself. The increase in potential spoils is brought about by modernization in all its forms, from communization (nationalization only brings more spoils to the private interests capturing the state) to de-communization (non-competitive privatization offers again great opportunity for spoiling). But the reduction of power discretion is anything but guaranteed. If many countries hold elections, more even than before, the accountability of rulers is still more of a desiderate than a reality even in such settings, let alone in autocracies.

Corruption at the individual level has been attributed, as have other criminal activities, to individuals' weighting of the expected costs and benefits of their actions in a given context and making their decisions on how to act 'not because their basic motivation differs from other persons but because their benefits and costs differ.' (Becker (1968, p. 176). Following Becker, other macro and micro level studies of corruption have advanced the idea of control of corruption as a balance between resources and costs (Becker and Stigler 1974; Nye 1967; Klitgaard 1998; Rose-Ackerman 1999; Huther and Shah 2000; Aidt 2003). When costs are low and opportunities are high, it is rational for individuals to be corrupt; especially if those around them behave similarly. Most individuals just follow the existing rules of the game rather than dissenting (Karklins 2005; della Porta and Vannucci 1999). But that structure of opportunities and penalties can eventually change, as winners and losers cannot go on eternally in a sustainable way. Even if that seems an insurmountable obstacle to change, dividing public resources always to the advantage of spoilers and managing to buy off eventual dissenters is sustainable only when unlimited resources exist (for instance, spoils from natural resources can be spread widely in exchange for political support through what are known as 'clientelist' policies). It seems therefore that governance evolves only incrementally and can be described as a series of equilibria.

The understanding of corruption as an equilibrium was pioneered by World Bank scholars. Robert Klitgaard (1988, p. 75) first developed this idea, which was later developed at the macro level by Huther and Shah (2000). Klitgaard proposed the following formula:

Corruption = Monopoly + Discretion − Accountability (C=M+D-A)

This formula expresses that corruption emerges when someone has monopoly power over a good or service, the discretion to decide who receives it and is not accountable. The logical solution that seems to derive from here is that corruption can be controlled by reducing or carefully regulating monopolies, curtailing official discretion and enhancing transparency (Klitgaard 1998, p. 4). Also, the probability of being caught should increase. There is only one problem when this model is considered in a given social context, which is that the principal who should enforce all this against the unruly agent is seldom there.

The ideal model to explain control of corruption should be an equilibrium model without a principal agent perspective. What such a model would measure is the collective capacity to enforce governance based on ethical universalism - any deviation from it creating social loss and discrimination. Empirical literature has, in fact, ample evidence to support such a model, although the idea of this holistic approach to a causal model was advanced only recently (Mungiu-Pippidi et al. 2011). Factors could be grouped thus:

Under opportunities or *resources*:
- **Discretionary power resources** due not only to monopoly, but also to privileged access under power arrangements other than monopoly or oligopoly – for example, status groups (Weber 1978), negative social capital networks (Olson 1965), and social orders, cartels, etc. (North et al. 2009).
- **Material resources**, such as state assets and discretionary budget spending, foreign aid, natural resources (resource curse), public sector employment, preferential legislation to influence markets (Johnston 2006) and any other resources which can be turned into spoils or generate rents.

Under deterrents or constraints:
- **Legal constraints**, supposing an autonomous, accountable, and effective judiciary able to enforce legislation, as well as a body of effective and comprehensive laws, with control agencies able to monitor their implementation.
- **Normative constraints,** which implies that existing societal norms endorse ethical universalism and permanently as well as effectively monitor deviations from that norm (through public opinion, media, civil society, critical citizens/voters etc). For an effective sanction we need a population of autonomous and critical citizens capable of collective action, not a mass of citizens merely conforming to the corrupt rules of the game.

Control of corruption or its antithesis, particularism, could thus be summarized in the following formula:

Control of corruption = Opportunities (Power discretion + Material resources) – Constraints (Legal + Normative)

This equilibrium formula can be tested empirically and offers a more complex picture, not only of the individual causes of corruption (or even categories of factors), but also of their interaction, which allows for a better understanding of why certain policy combinations work and others do not. All elements of the formula can be affected by human agency. Resources, for example, are not an absolute given; they can be manipulated by policy. Power resources can be increased by discretionary regulation and red tape and decreased by transparency; many anti-corruption policies focus on that area.

Opportunities can include a number of things, for example natural resources in state property, foreign aid (Easterly and Levine 1997) discretionary expenditures, public jobs, public contracts, preferential bailouts, subsidies, loans from state banks or any form of monetary rents, preferential concessions and privatizations of state property, and market advantages in the form of preferential regulation. Opportunities are a mixture of resources and the discretion to allow them to be used for rent creation. In bivariate models economies based on fuel or aid are indeed associated with greater corruption, but in more complex models direct material resources lose their significance- they seem to be a 'curse' only in very poor dependent societies, which in itself is problematic and increases the responsibility of Western donors or companies acting in such environments. Government investment in capital formation is a stable finding. Countries, which spend more on 'projects', either in the EU or in developing countries, tend to exert less control over corruption.

Some economists have argued that government intervention in the economy only creates resources for corruption. Vito Tanzi (1994), for example, suggests that government intervention in free markets creates rents and leads to a sharp rise in corruption payments. Several papers on trade agreements and aid present evidence that control of corruption is associated with more economic freedom, less regulation and more competition (Ades and Di Tella 1999). Kaufmann (1997) tests the relationship between an indicator of regulatory discretion and corruption and finds a strong correlation in a small sample of developing countries. Power discretion is actually a robust determinant of corruption whatever the proxy used, but economic freedom (i.e. proxies used by either the Fraser Institute or Heritage Foundation) and red tape (cf. World Bank Ease of Doing Business) are especially robust predictors of it (**Figure 5** and **Figure 6**).

Husted (1999) tested a more specific 'power distance' – the extent to which less powerful members of society expect and accept unequal influence – and found it positively associated with corruption, as were the extent of dominance of materialism and the perceived threat of uncertainty. That finding greatly supports the idea that social conformity allows power discretion in societies dominated by particularism, but such surveys exist for only a limited number of countries.

Figure 5. Association between control of corruption and economic freedom.

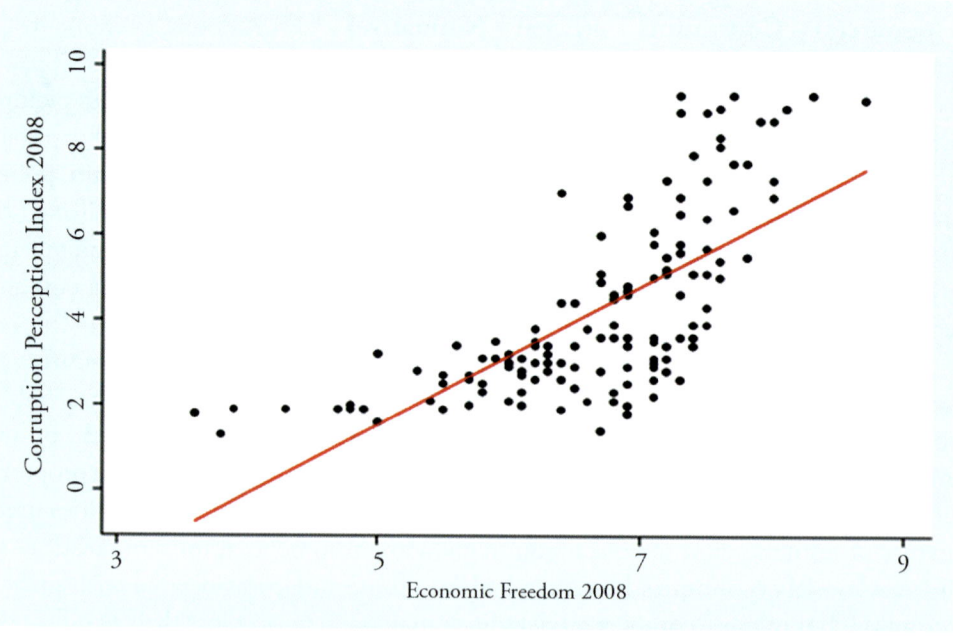

Source: Transparency International, CPI (10 = less corrupt) and Fraser Institute, Economic Freedom of the World Index (10 = more economic freedom).

Figure 6. Association between control of corruption and red tape.

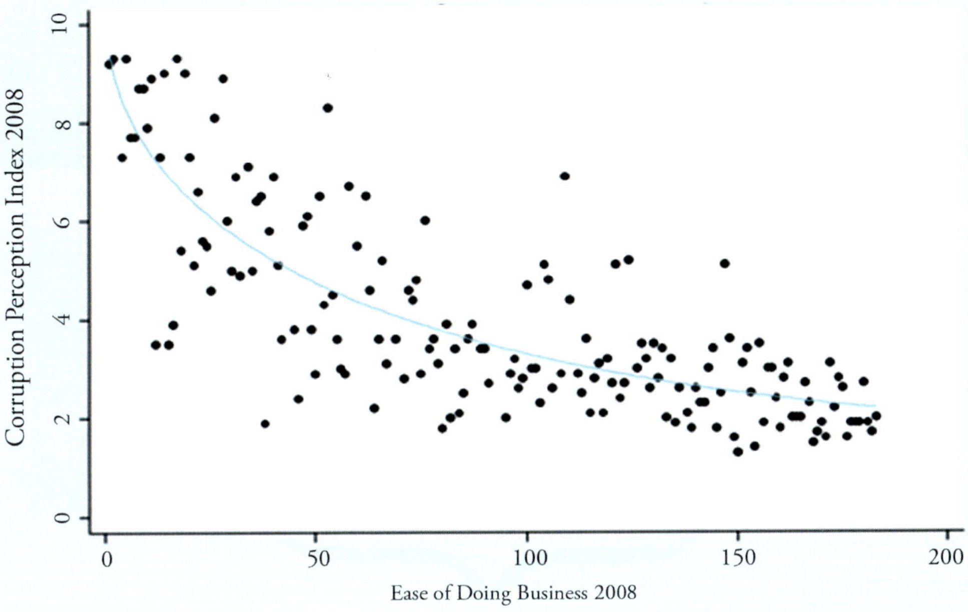

Source: Transparency International, CPI (10 = less corrupt) and World Bank, Ease of Doing Business Index (1 = most business friendly).

Economic freedom and red tape figures (**Figure 5** and **Figure 6**) illustrate how power and material resources interact, for instance rulers promoting regulations that only increase their discretionary power and create resources for their own further spoiling. Discretionary regulation offering opportunities for extortion can be promoted under any regime – by a group of parties just as well as by a dictator. Thus, proxies for political determinants become insignificant when tested in the same time period in the model. Since all variables are interconnected and some basic modernization factors influence many of them, a path model is needed to illustrate their relationships. **Figure 7** illustrates such a model.

The equilibrium model should not, however, be understood in terms of separate variables or even groups of them, but as a complex mechanism. More discretionary resources in the hands of a corrupt government only increases corruption, but once the equilibrium is reached where corruption is controlled, it is possible that if more spending is dedicated to welfare social trust is increased and will play a very positive role (Tanzi and Davoodi 1998; Rothstein and Uslaner 2005). It is not the volume of government spending, but the discretion of spending which matters.

Figure 7. Theoretical path model of control of corruption.

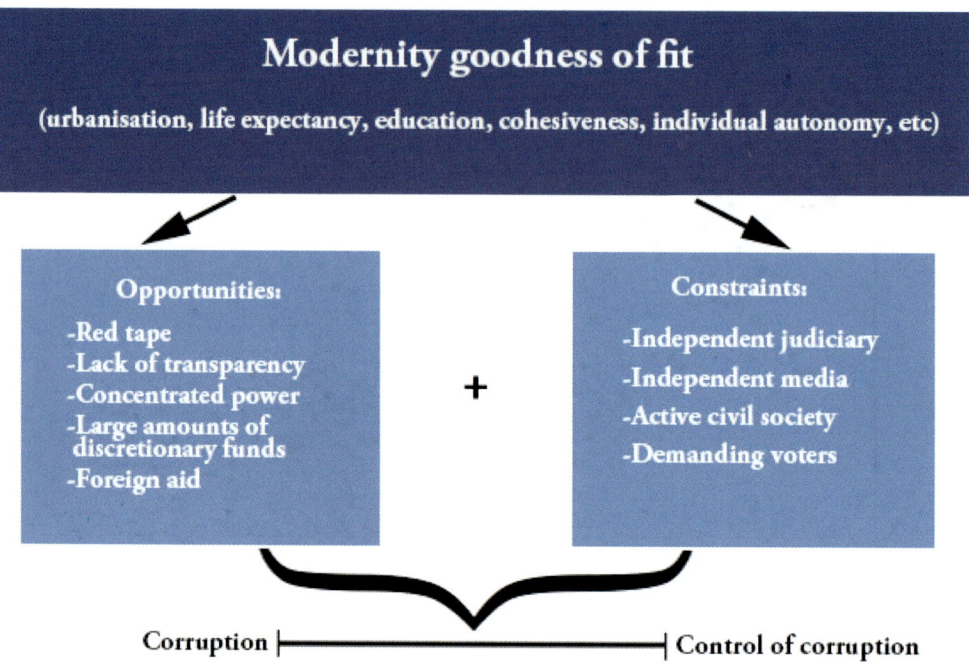

Constraints, on the other hand, have to be seen as societal constraints to be truly independent of the core cause of particularism, which is inequality between public influence resources which generates uneven access to public rents. In other words, the government should not be expected to constrain itself through an autonomous bureaucracy. The existence of an autonomous bureaucracy is so much part of the definition of control of corruption that it should be considered to be part of the dependent variable and not truly an independent factor, so as not to enter the vicious circle of 'when the solution is the problem' described by development scholars (Pritchett and Woolcock 2004). In corrupt countries bureaucracies are entirely part of the problem through politicization, nepotism or patronage.

Could the same argument be made for the judiciary? Only to a limited extent; there exists the principle of separation of powers for judiciaries, presently enshrined in most Constitutions, but which does not exist for bureaucracies and which matters both in constitutional and practical terms (recruitment, dismissal). A bureaucracy, regardless of how it is organized, exists to implement a government's will, so in the end it is prevented from being truly 'autonomous'. The judiciary is there to control government and few governments still have direct appointment powers. Of course, the government has other tools to prevent the judiciary from censoring it; still the distance is greater than in the case of bureaucracy and other factors than government intervene in shaping an autonomous judiciary (Neild 2002).

Judiciary can be independent, but still corrupt: a good performance measure of the judiciary must look at its accountability, not just its independence (for instance, tenure), a measure already covered by power discretion. We find a strong association, as expected, between autonomy of the judiciary and control of corruption, an expert score compiled by World Economic Forum (conceiving independence from private interest also, not just politics). That score is a highly significant and robust determinant of control of corruption, and the significance of the judiciary performance has been previously reported (cf. Messick 1999; Damania et al. 2004; Ali and Isse 2003; Brunetti and Weder 2003; Herzfeld and Weiss 2003; Park 2003; Broadman and Recanatini 2000; Leite and Weidmann 1999; Ades and Di Tella 1997). However, due to the high discretion of the nature of its activity the judiciary remains in practice one of the most difficult areas for external donors to treat, so there is a great distance from its significance to some meaningful recommendations (Fukuyama 2004).

Any model explaining control of corruption – no matter how carefully built and tested – is bound to be reductionist. **Figure 7** suggests that the broader development and stability context influences nearly all factors in the equilibrium equation and can, in turn, be influenced by many of them in the long run. The 'equilibrium' model builds on the modernization model, but departs from it in that all its factors can be influenced by human agency. However, its empirical validation proves to be challenging. The complex associations of variables make it difficult to find clearly distinguishable indicators for each of them. As a result, serious co-linearity problems may arise. In addition, the absence of time series for appropriate indicators renders such an empirical path model hardly feasible. On the hand, a simplified cross-sectional model may also raise potential endogeneity problems.

Table 9 proposes however a parsimonious model, which seems robust across our three different measures of corruption (aggregate score, business survey, general population survey). As proxies we used:

- For power discretion, the score of physical integrity rights;
- For administrative discretion, the ease of doing business (also, services offered as e-government and other transparency indicators, economic freedom, economic globalization index);
- For factionalism, ethnic fractionalization;
- For material resources, an indicator on abundance on natural resources. Other indicators can be amount of spending going into procurement (this data is difficult to find for many countries, but for the EU-28, where data is available, the effect of the variable is significant) or amount of assistance funds as percentage of GDP;
- For legal constraints, the expert score produced by the World Economic Forum on Judicial Independence;
- For normative constraints, the determinants tested were press freedom, civil society (measured in simple numbers of CSOs per 100,000 inhabitants) and Internet access (signifying the presence of well-informed and therefore potentially critical citizens), social and communication globalization index.

The parsimonious cross-sectional 'equilibrium' model (see **Table 9**) proved to be robust, highly significant and with high explanatory power in the dataset with little variation from one model to another and controlling for development as well as regional differences[4]. Additional to independent judiciary system and lack of power discretion, civil society, press freedom and the existence of enlightened citizens (newspaper readership, Internet connections) positively influence control of corruption. In particular, press freedom and civil society have previously been reported to be significant by Brunetti and Weider (2003); Grimes (2008) and Mungiu-Pippidi (2012).

As mentioned above, testing the model predictions with time series data we have to use different indicators compared to those that have been used with cross-country analysis due to lack of availability of certain variables. In particular, the estimation models presented in **Table 12** introduce two new indicators, which have not been used in the previous analysis and are part of the so-called KOF Index of Globalization: one is a measure on the degree of economic globalization that captures trade as well as financial openness, and the second measures the degree of social openness that is mostly based on the data on information flows and usage of telecommunication services. The data covers the years 1996-2011 and a sample of 148 countries. We use 3-years averages to take the persistence of institutional indicators into account, and apply two standard estimation methods for panel data analysis: random effects model and fixed effects model. The latter one is used to additionally account for potential effects of country-specific unobserved time invariant factors such as political culture, tradition, etc. We include indicators for rural population and education to control for the effect of development because the data on HDI is not available annually. Furthermore, since the results might be driven by the inclusion of developed countries, columns (5)-(8) repeat the estimations from the previous four models considering only middle and low-income countries. Overall the models explain more than 70% of the differences in the level of control of corruption in our total data sample, most of which, however, resulting from the cross-country rather than time variation (which endorses the hypothesis that causes leading to evolution or change in control of corruption are different than causes explaining why in a given moment in time certain countries enjoy it and others not). Our general findings are consistent with those obtained from the cross-sectional analysis. In particular, the results show that power discretion and dependency on natural resource revenues tend to determine poor control of corruption. By contrast, economic openness, resulting in a higher degree of competitiveness, and normative constraints, captured by the degree of social openness as well as press freedom, positively influence control of corruption.

---

[4] When using the GCB measure on corruption as a dependent variable, regional dummies are not included because of the limited sample size. Furthermore, models IV-VIII additionally control for the effect of the squared term of the freedom of the press score due to its non-linear relationship with the respective corruption indicator.

Table 9. Equilibrium cross-sectional models.

VARIABLES	WGI Control on Corruption			WEF Diversion of public funds (1-7 very uncommon)			GCB % of respondents who consider public officials as corrupt	
	Model I	Model II	Model III	Model IV	Model V	Model VI	Model VII	Model VIII
Physical integrity index (0-8 best)	0.095***	0.095***	0.099***	0.086***	0.086***	0.094***	0.259	0.263
	(4.60)	(4.59)	(4.46)	(3.10)	(3.04)	(2.95)	(0.22)	(0.22)
Judicial independence (1-7 best)	0.391***	0.389***	0.305***	0.718***	0.716***	0.668***	-4.130**	-4.114**
	(14.17)	(13.75)	(7.66)	(14.65)	(14.47)	(11.86)	(-2.05)	(-2.03)
Ease of doing business rank (1-183 worst)	-0.002***	-0.003***	-0.003***	-0.003**	-0.003**	-0.004**	0.095*	0.096*
	(-3.00)	(-2.87)	(-3.52)	(-2.02)	(-2.06)	(-2.25)	(1.68)	(1.68)
Ethnic fractionalization	-0.022	-0.048	-0.038	0.015	-0.030	0.046	12.82	13.15
	(-0.15)	(-0.28)	(-0.27)	(0.08)	(-0.15)	(0.22)	(1.65)	(1.45)
Freedom of the press (1-100 most free)	0.005**	0.005**	0.004*	-0.036***	-0.035***	-0.028**	1.135**	1.128**
	(2.07)	(2.14)	(1.69)	(-3.44)	(-3.44)	(-2.39)	(2.24)	(2.14)
Freedom of the press (squared)				0.0002**	0.0002**	0.0002	-0.011**	-0.010**
				(2.12)	(2.09)	(1.40)	(-2.14)	(-2.06)
CSOs per capita	0.005**	0.005**	0.003	0.008**	0.008**	0.009***	-0.322**	-0.322**
	(2.58)	(2.54)	(1.64)	(2.56)	(2.52)	(2.82)	(-2.26)	(-2.24)
Internet access (per 100 people)	0.007***	0.008***	0.010***	0.005**	0.007*	0.006	0.117	0.107
	(4.14)	(3.49)	(3.80)	(2.12)	(1.91)	(1.66)	(0.99)	(0.70)
Natural resources dummy	-0.109	-0.100	-0.121	-0.159*	-0.144	-0.132	6.217*	6.078
	(-1.32)	(-1.18)	(-1.60)	(-1.67)	(-1.47)	(-1.30)	(1.72)	(1.63)
HDI		-0.192	0.448		-0.317	-0.601		2.386
		(-0.48)	(0.77)		(-0.57)	(-0.85)		(0.11)
Asia and the Pacific			-0.037			-0.232		
			(-0.19)			(-0.91)		
Eastern Europe and the Baltics			-0.486***			-0.516***		
			(-4.18)			(-2.73)		
Former Soviet Union			-0.294*			-0.148		
			(-1.74)			(-0.58)		
Latin America			0.0214			-0.343		
			(0.14)			(-1.50)		
The Caribbean			-0.684***			-0.728**		
			(-3.35)			(-2.51)		
Middle East and North Africa			-0.094			-0.110		
			(-0.64)			(-0.48)		
Sub-Saharan Africa			0.196			-0.373		
			(1.00)			(-1.30)		
Constant	-2.277***	-2.150***	-2.207***	1.516***	1.697***	2.119***	31.42*	30.10
	(-12.39)	(-6.12)	(-5.31)	(3.36)	(2.87)	(2.99)	(1.67)	(1.38)
Countries	123	123	123	123	123	123	85	85
Adj. R-squared	0.90	0.90	0.93	0.88	0.88	0.89	0.44	0.43

OLS regressions using data for 2010. GCB data is for 2012. Data on CSOs numbers and ethnic fractionalization stem from 2008 and 2001, respectively. Robust standard errors are used; t statistics in parentheses / *** $p<0.01$, ** $p<0.05$, * $p<0.10$

Table 10. Panel regressions.

VARIABLES	All countries						Middle and low income countries			
	RE	RE	FE	RE	FE	RE	RE	FE	RE	FE
Physical Integrity Index (0-8 best)	0.056***	0.056***	0.053***	0.049***	0.048***	0.046***	0.050***	0.046***
	(5.03)	(4.80)	(4.46)	(3.85)	(4.24)	(3.70)	(3.88)	(3.17)
Freedom of the Press (1-100 most free)	0.006***	0.008***	0.002	0.004	0.005***	0.007***	0.002	0.005**
	(3.69)	(4.03)	(1.22)	(1.47)	(2.95)	(3.33)	(1.27)	(1.98)
Social openness (1-100 most open)	0.019***	0.015***	0.009**	0.006	0.012***	0.011***	0.013***	0.012**
	(8.17)	(5.11)	(2.18)	(1.56)	(5.81)	(3.56)	(3.14)	(2.50)
Economic openness (1-100 most open)	0.006***	0.007***	0.006**	0.007***	0.005**	0.006**	0.005**	0.007**
	(3.29)	(3.23)	(2.61)	(2.67)	(2.58)	(2.54)	(2.15)	(2.09)
Natural resource rents (% GDP)	-0.073**	-0.068*	-0.083**	-0.089	-0.073**	-0.064*	-0.068	-0.058
	(-2.37)	(-1.79)	(-2.03)	(-1.59)	(-2.41)	(-1.81)	(-1.62)	(-1.04)
Rural population (% total pop.)		-0.005*		-0.002		0.001		0.000
		(-1.84)		(-0.28)		(0.44)		(0.02)
Tertiary school enrolment (% total pop.)		-0.000		-0.001		0.000		0.002
		(-0.13)		(-0.51)		(0.09)		(0.65)
Constant	-1.667***	-1.373***	-0.964***	-0.779	-1.377***	-1.541***	-1.331***	-1.525**
	(-12.19)	(-4.73)	(-4.37)	(-1.43)	(-10.25)	(-5.68)	(-6.53)	(-2.36)
Observations	724	525	724	525	559	384	559	384
Countries	148	137	148	137	121	111	121	111
R-squared (overall)	0.72	0.71	0.69	0.69	0.49	0.47	0.47	0.45
R-squared (within)	0.12	0.12	0.13	0.13	0.15	0.17	0.15	0.17

The dependent variable is "control of corruption" from WGI. The data sample consists of 3-year averages covering 1996-2011. By country clustered standard errors are used; t statistics in parentheses: * $p<0.1$ ** $p<0.05$ *** $p<0.01$. All regressions include period dummies

Conclusions

As is clear from the analysis above, only individual assessments can diagnose a specific country and find remedies and no universal silver bullet exists. Indeed, if the norm is not ethical universalism then the specific term 'anti-corruption' might even be inappropriate in itself. What is needed to achieve results in fighting corruption is complex state building and deep democratization, empowering those who lose from corruption under current institutions, the upsetting of the current equilibrium and the achievement of another, superior, equilibrium, in the medium- to long-term investment. Cases such as Uruguay, Costa Rica, Estonia and Georgia prove that it is possible.

A forecast based on this model would imply that change in governance order can occur only gradually and by a succession of radical actions and disequilibria until new equilibrium is achieved with better control of corruption. That explains why so few success stories exist, and why they seem to result more from domestic agency and broad reforms than from typical anti-corruption focused on repressive agencies.

Control of corruption in a society has to be understood as a complex balancing act rather than as a group of separate factors determining corruption. Therefore anti corruption (AC) cannot be effective unless it manages to assemble these features:

1. AC is adjusted to the real equilibrium level (particular transactions are either the exception or the norm) as two different sets of policies apply (contextual);
2. If particular transactions are widespread AC needs to affect more than one element (comprehensive);
3. If particular transactions are widespread, AC needs to be radical and strong enough to affect the balance and so trigger a disequilibrium (deep);
4. If particular transactions are widespread AC needs to involve both state (e.g. fiscal transparency) and society (watchdog NGOs) in order to influence both sides of the formula (balanced);
5. If particular transactions are widespread AC needs to result from action by those groups on all sides (state and society) who oppose the institutional status quo (genuine 'principals') and cannot be simply conceived as top-down 'reforms'.

References

Acemoglu, D. and Robinson, J. (2012) *Why Nations Fail: the Origins of Power, Prosperity, and Poverty*, New York: Crown Business

Ades, A. and Di Tella, R. (1997) 'The new economics of corruption: a survey and some new results', *Political Studies*, 45(3), pp. 496-515

Ades, A. and Di Tella, R. (1999) 'Rents, Competition, and Corruption', *The American Economic Review*, 89(4), pp. 982-94

Aidt, T. S. (2003) 'Economic analysis of corruption: a survey', *The Economic Journal*, 113, pp. 632–52

Ali, M. A. and Isse, H. S. (2003) 'Determinants of Economic Corruption: A Cross-Country Comparison', *Cato Journal*, 22(3), pp. 449-66

Andrews, M. (2008) 'The Good Governance Agenda: Beyond Indicators without Theory', *Oxford Development Studies*, 36(4), pp. 379–407

Ariu, A. and Squicciarini, M. P. (2013) 'The balance of brains – corruption and migration', *EMBO reports*, 14, pp. 502-04

Bac, M. (2001) 'Corruption, Connections and Transparency: Does a Better Screen Imply a Better Scene?' *Public Choice*, 107, pp. 87-96

Baker, R. and McKenzie, N. (2012) 'Labor rejects call for national corruption agency', *Sydney Morning Herald*, February 15

Banisar, D. (2006) *Freedom of Information around the World 2006: A Global Survey of Access to Government Information Laws*, London: Privacy International

Becker, G. (1968) 'Crime and Punishment: An Economic Approach', *The Journal of Political Economy*, 76, pp. 169–217

Becker, G. and Stigler, G. (1974) 'Law Enforcement, Malfeasance, and the Compensation of Enforcers', *Journal of Legal Studies*, 3, pp. 1-19

Broadman, H. G. and Recanatini, F. (2000) 'Seed of Corruption: Do Market Institutions Matter?' *The World Bank Policy Research Working Paper No. 2368*

Brown, A. J. and Head, B. (2004) 'Ombudsman, Corruption Commission or Police Integrity Authority? Choices for Institutional Capacity in Australia's Integrity Systems', Paper presented at the Australasian Political Studies Association Conference, Adelaide (29 Sept-1 Oct 2004)

Brown, D. S., Touchton, M. and Whitford, A. B. (2005) 'Political Polarizationas a Constraint on Government: Evidence from Corruption', Available from: <http://ssrn.com/abstract=782845>

Brunetti, A. and Weder, B. (2003) 'A Free Press is Bad News for Corruption', *Journal of Public Economics*, 87, pp. 1801-24

Chang, E. C. C. and Golden, M. A. (2004) 'Electoral Systems, District Magnitude and Corruption'. Paper presented at the 2003 annual meeting of the American Political Science Association (August 28-31, 2003)

Charron, N. (2013) 'European Perceptions of Quality of Government: A Survey of 24 Countries'. In A. Mungiu-Pippidi (ed.) *The Anti-corruption Report, Vol. 1: Controlling Corruption in Europe,* Berlin: Barbara Budrich Publishers, pp. 99-120

Charron, N., Lapuente, V. and Rothstein, B. (eds.) (2013) *Quality of Government and Corruption from a European Perspective: A Comparative Study of Good Government in EU Regions*, Edward Elgar Publishing

Cingranelli, D. L. and Richards, D. L. (2010) The Cingranelli-Richards (CIRI) Human Rights Dataset

Damania, R., Fredriksson, P. and Muthukumara, M. (2004) 'The Persistence of Corruption and Regulatory Compliance Failures: Theory and Evidence', *Public Choice*, 121, pp. 363-90

de Sousa, L. (2009) 'Anti-Corruption Agencies: Between Empowerment and Irrelevance', EUI Working Paper, RSCAS 2009/08

della Porta, D. and Vannucci, A. (1999) *Corrupt Exchanges: Actors, Resources, and Mechanisms of Political Corruption*, New York: Walter de Gruyter

Doig, A., Watt, D. and Williams, R. (2005) 'Measuring 'success' in five African Anti- Corruption Commissions, the cases of Ghana, Malawi, Tanzania, Uganda & Zambia', Bergen: U4

Dreher, A. (2006) 'Does Globalization Affect Growth? Evidence from a New Index of Globalization', *Applied Economics*, 38 (10), pp. 1091-100

Easterly, W. and Levine, R. (1997) 'Africa's Growth Tragedy: Policies and Ethnic Divisions', *Quarterly Journal of Economics*, 112(4), pp. 1203-50

Escaleras, M., Lin S. and Register, C. (2010) 'Freedom of information acts and public sector corruption', *Public Choice*, 145, pp. 435-60

Evans, P. (2004) 'Development as Institutional Change: The Pitfalls of Monocropping and the Potentials of Deliberation', *Studies in Comparative International Development*, 38(4), pp. 30-52

Fukuyama, F. (2004) *State Building: Governance and World Order in the 21st Century*, Ithaca, NY: Cornell University Press

GRECO (2009) Evaluation Report on Denmark on Incriminations (ETS 173 and 191, GPC 2), Adopted by GRECO at its 43rd Plenary Meeting. Available from: <http://www.coe.int/t/dghl/monitoring/greco/evaluations/round3/GrecoEval3per cent282008per cent299_Denmark_One_EN.pdf>

Grimes, M. (2009) 'The Role of Civil Society Organizations in Combating Corruption', Paper presented at the annual meeting of the MPSA Annual National Conference. Available from: <http://www.allacademic.com/meta/p266844_index.html>

Heilbrunn, J. R. (2004) 'Anti-Corruption Commissions: Panacea or Real Medicine to Fight Corruption?' World Bank Institute, Working Paper 37234

Herzfeld, T. and Weiss, C. (2003) 'Corruption and Legal (In)-Effectiveness: An Empirical Investigation', *European Journal of Political Economy*, 19, pp. 621-32

Holmberg, S., Rothstein, B. and Nasiritousi, N. (2009) 'Quality of government: what you get', *Annual Review of Political Science*, 12: pp. 135-61

Huntington, S. (1968) *Political Order in Changing Societies*, New Haven: Yale University Press

Husted, B. W. (1999) 'Wealth, culture, and corruption', *Journal of International Business Studies*, 3(2), pp. 339-59

Huther, J. and Shah, A. (2000) 'Anti-corruption Policies and Programs: A Framework for Evaluation', Policy Research Working Paper 2501, World Bank, Washington, DC

International Monetary Fund (2010) 'Managing Natural Resource Wealth (MNRW-TTF)', Program Document. Washington D.C.: International Monetary Fund

International Monetary Fund (2012) 'Macroeconomic Policy Framework for Resource-Rich Developing Countries', Washington D.C.: International Monetary Fund

Islam, R. (2006) 'Does More Transparency go along with Better Governance?' *Economics and Politics*, 18(2), pp. 121-67

Johnston, M. (2005) *Syndromes of Corruption: Wealth, Power and Democracy*, New York: Cambridge University Press

Johnston, M. (2006) 'From Thucydides to Mayor Daley: Bad Politics, and a Culture of Corruption', *Political Science and Politics*, 39, pp. 809-12

Karklins, R. (2005) *The System Made Me Do It: Corruption in Post-Communist Societies*, New York: M.E. Sharpe

Kaufmann, D. (1997) 'Corruption: The Facts', *Foreign Policy*, 107, pp. 114-31

Kaufmann, D. (1998) 'Revisiting Anti-Corruption Strategies: Tilt Towards Incentive-Driven Approaches', Corruption & Integrity Improvement Initiatives in Developing Countries, UNDP

Klitgaard, R. (1988) *Controlling Corruption*. Berkley CA: University of California Press

Klitgaard, R (1998) 'International Cooperation against Corruption', *Finance and Development*, 35(1), pp. 3-6

Kocaoglu, N. and Figari, A. (2006) *Using the Right to Information as an Anti-Corruption Tool*, Berlin: Transparency International

Kunicova, J. and Rose-Ackerman, S. (2005) 'Electoral Rules and Constitutional Structures as Constraints on Corruption', *British Journal of Political Science*, 35(4), pp. 573-606

Lambsdorff, J. (2008) *The organization of anti-corruption: Getting incentives right!* Passau: Universität Passau, Wirtschaftswiss. Fakultät

Lederman, D., Loayza, N. and Soares, R. (2005) 'Accountability and Corruption: Political Institutions Matter', *Economics and Politics*, 17, pp. 1-35

Leite, C, A. and Weidmann, J. (1999) 'Does Mother Nature Corrupt? Natural Resources, Corruption, and Economic Growth', Working paper WP/99/85, International Monetary Fund, Washington, DC

Meagher, P. (2005) 'Anti-Corruption Agencies: Rhetoric versus Reality', *Journal of Policy Reform*, 8(1), pp. 69-103

Messick, R. E. (1999) 'Judicial reform and economic development: a survey of the issues', *The World Bank Research Observer*, 14(1), pp. 117-36

Mungiu-Pippidi, A. (2007) 'EU Accession Is No 'End of history'', *Journal of Democracy*, 18(4), pp. 8-16

Mungiu-Pippidi, A. et al. (2011) Contextual Choices in Fighting Corruption: Lessons Learned, NORAD, Report 4/2011. Available from: <http://www.norad.no/en/tools-and-publications/publications/publication?key=383808>

Mungiu-Pippidi, A. (2012) 'Freedom without Impartiality: The Vicious Circle of Media Capture', in P. Gross and K. Jakubowicz (eds.), *Media Transformations in the Post-Communist World*, New York: Lexington Books, pp. 33-47

Mungiu-Pippidi, A. (2013) 'Global comparative trend analysis report', ANTICORRP project. Available from: <http://anticorrp.eu/publications/global-comparative-trend-analysis-report-1>

Mungiu-Pippidi, A. (2014) 'Becoming Denmark: Historical Designs of Corruption Control', *Social Research*, 80(4), pp. 1259-86

Neild, R. R. (2002) *Public corruption: The dark side of social evolution*, London: Anthem Press

North, D. C.; Wallis J. J. and Weingast, B. R. (2009) *Violence and Social Orders: A Conceptual Framework for Interpreting Recorded Human History*, New York: Cambridge University Press

Nye, J. S. (1967) 'Corruption and Political Development: A Cost-Benefit Analysis', *American Political Science Review*, 61(2), pp. 417-27

Olson, M. (1965) *The logic of collective action: public goods and the theory of groups*, Cambridge: Harvard University Press

Park, H. (2003) 'Determinants of Corruption: A Cross-National Analysis', *The Multinational Business Review*, 11(2) pp. 29-48

Persson, T. and Tabellini, G. (2004) 'Constitutions and Economic Policy', *The Journal of Economic Perspectives*, 18 (1), pp. 75-98

Persson, T. and Tabellini, G. E. (2003) *The economic effects of constitutions*, Cambridge, MA: MIT Press

Pierson, P. (2000) 'The limits of design: Explaining institutional origins and change', *Governance* 13(4), pp. 475-99

Pritchett, L. and Woolcock, M. (2004) 'Solutions When the Solution is the Problem: Arraying the Disarray in Development', *World Development*, 32(2), pp. 191-212

PRS (2013) ICRG Methodology. Available from: <http://www.prsgroup.com/ICRG_Methodology.aspx#PolRiskRating>

Rose-Ackerman, S. (1999) *Corruption and government: Causes, consequences, and reform*, London: Cambridge University Press

Rothstein, B. and Uslaner, E. M. (2005) 'All for All: Equality and Social Trust', *World Politics*, 58, pp. 41-72

Rothstein, B. and Teorell, J. (2011) *The Quality of Government: Corruption, Social Trust, and Inequality in International Perspective*, Chicago: The University of Chicago Press

Salamon, L. M., Sokolowski, S. W. and List, R. (2003) *Global Civil Society: An Overview*, The Johns Hopkins Comparative Nonprofit Sector Project

SAR (Romanian Academic Society) (2011) 'Beyond Perception: Has Romania's Governance Improve after 2004?' Annual Report of Romanian Academic Society. Available from: <http://www.sar.org.ro/files/Corruption.pdf>

Sartori, G. (1994) *Comparative constitutional engineering: An inquiry into structures, incentives, and outcomes*, New York: New York University Press

Scott, J. C. (1972) *Political Corruption*, Englewood Cliffs, N.J.: Prentice-Hall

Tanzi, V. (1994) 'Corruption, Governmental Activities and Markets', IMF Working Paper 94/99, International Monetary Fund, Washington, DC

Tanzi, V. and Davoodi, H. R. (1997) 'Corruption, Public Investment, and Growth', IMF Working Paper 97/139

Treisman, D. (2000) 'The causes of corruption: a cross-national study', *Journal of Public Economics*, 76(3), pp. 399-457

UNDP (2005) Institutional Arrangements to Combat Corruption – A Comparative Study, UNDP Democratic Governance Practice Team

USAID (2006) Anti-corruption Agencies (ACAs): Office of Democracy and Governance Anti-corruption Program Brief. USAID

van Aaken, A., Feld, L. and Voigt, S., (2008) 'Power over Prosecutors Corrupts Politicians: Cross Country Evidence Using a New Indicator,' CESifo Working Paper No. 2245

Vleugels, R. (2008) Overview of all 86 FOIA countries, Dataset: 18. Available from: <http://right2info.org/resources/publications/Fringepercent20Specialpercent20-per cent20Overviewpercent20FOIApercent20-percent20seppercent2020percent202010.pdf/view>

Wallace, C. and Haerpfer, C. W. (2000) 'Democratisation, Economic Development and Corruption in East-Central Europe', *Sociological Studies* 44. Vienna: Höhere Studien (IHS), Wien Institute for Advanced Studies

Weber, M. (1978) *Economy and Society*, Berkeley: University of California Press

World Bank (2011) 'Country-Level Engagement on Governance and Anti-corruption: An Evaluation of the 2007 Strategy and Implementation Plan', Washington, DC: Independent Evaluation Group, The World Bank Group

Appendix

Variable	Variable description / Measurement	Scale	Time period	Country coverage	Source
per cent of respondents who consider civil servants / public officials as corrupt	Percentage of respondents who answered the question: 'To what extent do you see public officials/civil servants to be affected by corruption in this country?' with 4 (corrupt) or 5 (extremely corrupt).	per cent	2012	110	Global Corruption Barometer 2012
Civil Society Organizations (number)	Data on the number of civil society organizations from CIVICUS, a global network of civil society organizations active in the area of social and economic development. The directory is compiled for the development community and does not purport to be an exhaustive register of all organizations. Grimes (2009) validated the data by comparing it to the results of a comprehensive analysis conducted at the Johns Hopkins University Center for Civil Society Studies of a much smaller subset of countries . Though the latter employs a broader definition of civil society and measures civil society as the proportion of a country's workforce active in civil society, the Johns Hopkins and CIVCUS measures correlate respectably (Pearson's r=0.63, p<0.001, N=35)	Numerical (0 to ∞)	2000	191	Grimes (2009) and Salamon et al. (2003)
Civil Society Organizations per million inhabitants	Number of civil society organizations per million inhabitants. For more information on the construction of the variable see 'Civil Society Organizations (number)' above.	Numerical (0 to ∞)	2000	191	Quality of Government Dataset
Diversion of public funds	In your country, how common is diversion of public funds to companies, individuals, or groups due to corruption?	1 (very common) - 7 (never occurs)	2010	135	Global Competitiveness Report
Ease of doing business	Ease of doing business ranks economies from 1 to 183, with first place being the best. A high ranking (a low Numerical (0 to ∞) rank) means that the regulatory environment is conducive to business operation. The index averages the country's percentile rankings on 10 topics covered in the World Bank's Doing Business. The ranking on each topic is the simple average of the percentile rankings on its component indicators.	1 (best)- 183 (worst)	2010	183	World Bank Database
Economic Openness Index	Economic globalization is characterized as long distance flows of goods and services as well as information and perceptions that accompany market exchanges	0 (least globalized)- 100 (most globalized)	1970-2010	207	Dreher (2006)
Ethnic fractionalization	Reflects probability that two randomly selected people from a given country will not belong to the same ethnolinguistic group. The higher the number, the more fractionalized society. The definition of ethnicity involves a combination of racial and linguistic characteristics.	0 (no fractionalization) - 1 (total fractionalization)	2001	183	Quality of Government Dataset
FOIA presence	Whether FOIA was in power this year	1 (FOIA is present) and 0 (no FOIA present)	2010	189	Hertie School of Governance database

Variable	Variable description / Measurement	Scale	Time period	Country coverage	Source
FOIA year	Year FOIA came into power	Numerical (0 to ∞)	2010	81	Hertie School of Governance database
Freedom of the Press	The press freedom index is computed by adding three component ratings: Laws and regulations, Political pressures and controls, Economic Influences and repressive actions.	0 (most free)- 100 (least free) or reversed scale when specified	2010	189	Freedom House
HDI	Summary composite index that measures a country's average achievements in three basic aspects of human development: longevity; knowledge, and a decent standard of living. Longevity is measured by life expectancy at birth; knowledge is measured by a combination of the adult literacy rate and the combined primary, secondary, and tertiary gross enrolment ratio; and standard of living is measured by GDP per capita. The Human Development Index (HDI), reported in the Human Development Report of the United Nations, is an indication of where a country is development wise. The index can take value between 0 and 1. Countries with an index over 0.800 are part of the High Human Development group. Between 0.500 and 0.800, countries are part of the Medium Human Development group and below 0.500 they are part of the Low Human Development group.	0 (lowest human development) to 1 (highest human development)	2010	185	UNDP database
Internet users (per 100 people)	Internet users (per 100 people)	per cent	2010	192	World Bank Database
Judicial independence	To what extent is the judiciary in your country independent from influences of members of government, citizens, or firms? [1 = heavily influenced; 7 = entirely independent]	1 (heavily influenced- 7 (entirely independent)	2010	135	Global Competitiveness Report
Natural resources rents	Total natural resources rents are the sum of oil rents, natural gas rents, coal rents (hard and soft), mineral rents, and forest rents.	%	1996-2011	196	World Bank Database
Natural resource dummy	Binary variable taking the value of 1 if a country is resource-rich according to the IMF classification: A country is classified as resource-rich if its natural resources contribute to at least 20% of its total fiscal revenues and/or at least 20% of its total exports.	1 (resource rich) and 0 (not resource rich)	1996-2011	196	IMF (2010) and IMF (2012)

Variable	Variable description / Measurement	Scale	Time period	Country coverage	Source
OBI (Open Budget Index)	The Open Budget Index rates countries on how open their budget books are to their citizens. It is intended to provide citizens, legislators, and civil society advocates with the comprehensive and practical information needed to gauge a government's commitment to budget transparency and accountability.	0 (scant or no information available)- 100 (extensive information available)	2010	100	Open Budget Survey 2010
Ombudsman presence	Whether ombudsman was in operation the previous year	1 (ombudsman is present) and 0 (no ombudsman is present)	2010	194	Hertie School of Governance database
Ombudsman year of creation	Year ombudsman started operating	Numerical (0 to ∞)	2010	131	Hertie School of Governance database
Physical integrity rights index	This is an additive index constructed from the Torture, Extrajudicial Killing, Political Imprisonment, and Disappearance indicators.	0 (no government respect for physical integrity) to 8 (full government respect to physical integrity)	2002-2010	187	Cingranelli and Richards (2010)
Presence of Anti-Corruption Agency (ACA)	Whether Anti-corruption Agency (ACA) was in operation the previous year	1 (ACA is present) and 0 (ACA is not present)	2010	171	Hertie School of Governance database
Risk of corruption	This is an assessment of corruption within the political system reported in a scale from 0 (lowest risk of corruption) to 6 (highest risk of corruption). The most common form of corruption met directly by business is financial corruption in the form of demands for special payments and bribes connected with import and export licenses, exchange controls, tax assessments, police protection, or loans. This measure takes such corruption into account, but it is more concerned with actual or potential corruption in the form of excessive patronage, nepotism, job reservations, 'favour-for-favours', secret party funding, and suspiciously close ties between politics and business. In our view these insidious sorts of corruption are potentially of much greater risk to foreign business in that they can lead to popular discontent, unrealistic and inefficient controls on the state economy, and encourage the development of the black market.	0 (lowest risk of corruption - 6 (highest risk of corruption)	1984-2012	139	PRS Group (ICRG)

Variable	Variable description / Measurement	Scale	Time period	Country coverage	Source
Rural population	% of total population living in rural areas	%	2010	210	World Bank Database
Social Openness index	Social globalization is expressed as the spread of ideas, information, images and people.	1 (least globalized) - 100 (most globalized)	1970-2010	207	Dreher (2006)
Tertiary school enrolment	Total enrolment in tertiary education, regardless of age, expressed as a percentage of the total population of the five-year age group following on from secondary school leaving.	%	2010	156	UNESCO Institute for Statistics
UNCAC year of ratification	Year of UNCAC ratification	Numerical (0 to ∞)	2010	147	Hertie School of Governance database
WGI Control of Corruption estimate	'Control of Corruption' measures perceptions of corruption, conventionally defined as the exercise of public power for private gain. The particular aspect of corruption measured by the various sources differs somewhat, ranging from the frequency of 'additional payments to get things done', to the effects of corruption on the business environment, to measuring 'grand corruption' in the political arena or in the tendency of elite forms to engage in 'state capture'. Estimate of governance (ranges from approximately -2.5 (weak) to 2.5 (strong) governance performance). The recoded version of this variable to a scale of 1 (lowest Control of Corruption) to 10 (highest control of corruption) was also used throughout this report.	-2.5 (weak control of corruption) -2.5 (strong control of corruption) (Alternatively recoded to a scale from 1 (lowest control of corruption) -10(highest control of corruption)	1996-2011	200	Worldwide Governance Indicators
WGI Political Stability estimate	Reflects perceptions of the likelihood that the government will be destabilized or overthrown by unconstitutional or violent means, including politically-motivated violence and terrorism. Estimate of governance (ranges from approximately -2.5 (weak) to 2.5 (strong) governance performance)	-2.5 (worst political stability) to 2.5 (best political stability)	2010	203	Worldwide Governance Indicators
Year of creation of the Anti-Corruption Agency (ACA)	Year when ACA was created	Numerical (0 to ∞)	2010	171	Hertie School of Governance database
Years since ACA was established	Years since ACA was established	Numerical (0 to ∞)	2010	171	Hertie School of Governance database
Years since FOIA came into power	Years since FOIA came into power	Numerical (0 to ∞)	2010	189	Hertie School of Governance database

Acknowledgments

This project is co-funded by the Seventh Framework Programme
for Research and Technological Development of the European Union

This policy report, The Anticorruption Report 2: The Anticorruption Frontline, is the second volume of the policy series "The Anticorruption Report" produced in the framework of the EU FP7 ANTICORRP Project. The report was edited by Prof. Dr. Alina Mungiu-Pippidi from the Hertie School of Governance, head of the policy pillar of the project.

ANTICORRP is a large-scale research project funded by the European Commission's Seventh Framework Programme. The full name of the project is "Anti-corruption Policies Revisited: Global Trends and European Responses to the Challenge of Corruption". The project started in March 2012 and will last for five years. The research is conducted by 21 research groups in sixteen countries.

The fundamental purpose of ANTICORRP is to investigate and explain the factors that promote or hinder the development of effective anti-corruption policies and impartial government institutions. A central issue is how policy responses can be tailored to deal effectively with various forms of corruption. Through this approach ANTICORRP seeks to advance the knowledge on how corruption can be curbed in Europe and elsewhere. Special emphasis is laid on the agency of different state and non-state actors to contribute to building good governance.

> Project acronym: ANTICORRP
> Project full title: Anti-corruption Policies Revisited: Global Trends and European Responses to the Challenge of Corruption
> Project duration: March 2012 – February 2017
> EU funding: Approx. 8 million Euros
> Theme: FP7-SSH.2011.5.1-1
> Grant agreement number: 290529
> Project website: http://anticorrp.eu/
> Full-length versions of Chapters 2, 3, 4, 5 and 6 are available at http://anticorrp.eu and www.againstcorruption.eu.

All these contributions were given as part of the European Union Seventh Framework Research Project ANTICORRP (Anti-corruption Policies Revisited: Global Trends and European Responses to the Challenge of Corruption). The views expressed in this report are solely those of the authors and the European Union is not liable for any use that may be made of the information contained therein.